Embers
99 Culinary Delights Inspired by the Menu of Asador Etxebarri, Axpe, Spain

Austria Tafelspitz Boiled Beef

Copyright © 2023 Austria Tafelspitz Boiled Beef
All rights reserved.
:

Contents

INTRODUCTION 8
1. Grilled Wild Mushrooms 10
2. Ember-Roasted Sea Urchin 11
3. Slow-Cooked Egg with White Truffle 13
4. Wood-Grilled Oysters 14
5. Fire-Grilled Caviar 16
6. Smoked Butter 17
7. Grilled Razor Clams 19
8. Charcoal-Grilled White Asparagus 20
9. Roasted Spring Onions 22
10. Ember-Grilled Palamós Prawns 24
11. Grilled Squid with Ink Sauce 25
12. Grilled Baby Leeks 26
13. Ember-Cooked Scarlet Shrimp 28
14. Oak-Grilled Artichokes 30
15. Grilled Cuttlefish 31
16. Wood-Fired Piquillos Peppers 33
17. Ember-Grilled Scallops 34
18. Grilled Octopus 35
19. Fire-Roasted Red Prawns 37
20. Whole Grilled Lobster 39
21. Ember-Grilled Langoustines 40
22. Oak-Smoked Foie Gras 42
23. Grilled Bonito Fish 43
24. Ember-Cooked Sardines 45
25. Grilled Mackerel with Green Pepper 46
26. Wood-Grilled Turbot 48
27. Ember-Roasted Monkfish 49

28. Charcoal-Grilled Hake 51

29. Grilled Sea Bass with Herbs 53

30. Oak-Grilled Sole 54

31. Ember-Cooked Codfish 56

32. Grilled Red Mullet 57

33. Fire-Grilled Grouper 59

34. Ember-Roasted John Dory 60

35. Oak-Grilled Salmon 62

36. Grilled Wild Trout 63

37. Wood-Grilled Eel 65

38. Ember-Grilled Anchovies 66

39. Grilled Mussels with Seaweed 68

40. Smoked Herring 69

41. Charcoal-Grilled Oily Fish Salad 71

42. Grilled Iberian Ham 73

43. Oak-Smoked Chorizo 74

44. Ember-Roasted Blood Sausage 75

45. Grilled Morcilla 77

46. Fire-Grilled Txistorra 78

47. Wood-Grilled Lamb Chops 80

48. Ember-Cooked Pork Ribs 81

49. Grilled Duck Breast 83

50. Oak-Grilled Quail 84

51. Ember-Roasted Pigeon 86

52. Grilled Rabbit with Garlic 87

53. Charcoal-Grilled Venison 89

54. Wood-Grilled Wild Boar 91

55. Ember-Cooked Beef Tenderloin 92

56. Grilled Iberian Pork 94

57. Oak-Grilled Ox Tongue 95

58. Ember-Roasted Sweetbreads 97

59. Grilled Bone Marrow 98

60. Wood-Grilled Veal Chop 100

61. Ember-Cooked Lamb Kidneys 101

62. Grilled Chicken Thighs 103

63. Fire-Grilled Turkey 105

64. Oak-Grilled Pheasant 106

65. Ember-Roasted Guinea Fowl 108

66. Grilled Duck Liver 109

67. Charcoal-Grilled Poultry Hearts 111

68. Wood-Grilled Poultry Gizzards 112

69. Ember-Cooked Escargot 114

70. Grilled Razor Shell Clams 116

71. Oak-Smoked Eel 117

72. Ember-Roasted Goose Liver 119

73. Grilled Baby Octopus 120

74. Fire-Grilled Abalone 121

75. Wood-Grilled Lobster Tail 123

76. Ember-Grilled King Crab Legs 124

77. Grilled Squat Lobster 126

78. Oak-Grilled Prawn Skewers 127

79. Ember-Roasted Sea Bass Fillet 129

80. Charcoal-Grilled Arctic Char 130

81. Grilled Turbot with Green Sauce 132

82. Wood-Grilled Dover Sole 133

83. Ember-Cooked Halibut 135

84. Grilled Red Mullet Fillet 136

85. Fire-Grilled Swordfish 138

86. Ember-Roasted Haddock 139
87. Oak-Grilled Pike Perch 141
88. Grilled Zander Fillet 142
89. Charcoal-Grilled Salmon Roe 144
90. Wood-Grilled Sturgeon 145
91. Ember-Cooked Cobia 147
92. Grilled Herring Roe 148
93. Fire-Grilled Trout Roe 150
94. Ember-Roasted Tobiko 151
95. Oak-Grilled Smelt Roe 153
96. Grilled Sea Urchin Roe 154
97. Wood-Grilled Mullet Roe 156
98. Ember-Cooked Flying Fish Roe 157
99. Charcoal-Grilled Lumpfish Roe 159
CONCLUSION 161

INTRODUCTION

Nestled in the picturesque village of Axpe, Spain, lies the culinary haven of Asador Etxebarri. Renowned for its commitment to the art of grilling and the sheer simplicity of its ingredients, this rustic gem has become an epicenter for gastronomic pilgrimage. Embers of Etxebarri is a celebration of the soul-stirring cuisine that emanates from the hearth of this revered establishment, offering 99 delectable recipes that encapsulate the essence of this culinary treasure.

Asador Etxebarri, under the skillful guidance of chef Victor Arguinzoniz, has become a touchstone for those who seek culinary perfection. The restaurant is a testament to the belief that the most profound flavors can be coaxed from the simplest of ingredients when subjected to the alchemy of open flame and seasoned wood. Embers of Etxebarri is a curated collection of gastronomic delights inspired by the diverse and tantalizing menu of this Michelin-starred establishment.

The heart and soul of Asador Etxebarri lie in its unwavering commitment to time-honored traditions, celebrating the primal art of grilling that goes back centuries. The recipes within these pages draw inspiration from the embers that dance beneath the grill grates, infusing each dish with a distinctive smokiness and an unmistakable depth of flavor. From succulent cuts of locally sourced meats to vibrant, charred vegetables, each recipe is a tribute to the elemental beauty of fire-kissed cuisine.

Embers of Etxebarri opens its doors to a world of culinary exploration, inviting both novice cooks and seasoned chefs alike to embark on a journey through the rich tapestry of flavors that define Basque Country's gastronomy. The recipes, carefully curated and adapted for home kitchens, capture the essence of the Asador Etxebarri experience while offering a practical approach to recreating these masterpieces in your own abode.

This cookbook is more than just a compilation of recipes; it's a homage to the ethos of Asador Etxebarri. Each page invites you to savor the romance of grilling, the alchemy of smoke, and the symphony of flavors that unfold with every flicker of the flame. From the iconic Chuleta – a perfectly grilled ribeye steak – to the humble yet extraordinary Grilled Vegetables, every dish encapsulates the spirit of Axpe, weaving together tradition, innovation, and a profound respect for the ingredients.

Whether you are an aspiring home cook or a seasoned epicurean, Embers of Etxebarri beckons you to embark on a culinary odyssey. Immerse yourself in the world of Basque flavors, and let the embers of Asador Etxebarri ignite your passion for the elemental art of grilling. Get ready to transform your kitchen into a rustic haven where the spirit of Axpe comes alive in 99 tantalizing culinary delights.

1. Grilled Wild Mushrooms

Embark on a culinary journey inspired by the renowned menu of Asador Etxebarri in Axpe, Spain, with our tantalizing recipe for Grilled Wild Mushrooms. Elevate your taste buds with the smoky and robust flavors that pay homage to the exceptional grilling techniques of this distinguished establishment. Savor the essence of Spanish cuisine in the comfort of your own kitchen with this delectable dish.

Serving: 4 servings
Preparation Time: 15 minutes
Ready Time: 30 minutes

Ingredients:
- 1 pound wild mushrooms (such as chanterelles, shiitake, or oyster mushrooms), cleaned and sliced
- 3 tablespoons extra-virgin olive oil
- 2 cloves garlic, minced
- 1 tablespoon fresh thyme leaves
- Salt and black pepper, to taste
- 1 tablespoon balsamic vinegar
- Fresh parsley, chopped (for garnish)

Instructions:
1. Preheat the grill to medium-high heat.
2. In a large bowl, toss the wild mushrooms with olive oil, minced garlic, fresh thyme leaves, salt, and black pepper. Ensure the mushrooms are evenly coated with the flavorful mixture.
3. Place a grill basket or a sheet of aluminum foil directly on the grill grates. Spread the seasoned mushrooms evenly on the basket or foil.
4. Grill the mushrooms for about 15-20 minutes, turning occasionally, until they are tender and have a delightful smoky aroma.
5. Remove the mushrooms from the grill and transfer them to a serving platter.
6. Drizzle balsamic vinegar over the grilled mushrooms, giving them a subtle tangy kick.
7. Garnish with fresh chopped parsley for a burst of color and added freshness.

8. Serve the Grilled Wild Mushrooms as a savory side dish or as a tapas-style appetizer, allowing the flavors to shine.

Nutrition Information:
Note: Nutrition information is approximate and may vary based on specific mushroom varieties used.
- Calories: 120 per serving
- Total Fat: 9g
- Saturated Fat: 1.5g
- Cholesterol: 0mg
- Sodium: 150mg
- Total Carbohydrates: 8g
- Dietary Fiber: 2g
- Sugars: 3g
- Protein: 4g

Elevate your dining experience with this Grilled Wild Mushrooms recipe, capturing the essence of Asador Etxebarri's culinary excellence in every bite.

2. Ember-Roasted Sea Urchin

Embark on a culinary journey inspired by the renowned Restaurant Asador Etxebarri in Axpe, Spain, with our Ember-Roasted Sea Urchin recipe. This dish captures the essence of the restaurant's commitment to grilling and wood-fire cooking, creating a symphony of flavors that dance on your palate. Elevate your dining experience with this exquisite seafood delicacy, where the delicate taste of sea urchin meets the smoky embrace of ember-roasting.

Serving: 2 servings
Preparation Time: 15 minutes
Ready Time: 30 minutes

Ingredients:
- 8 fresh sea urchin roe (uni)
- 1/4 cup extra-virgin olive oil
- 1 tablespoon fresh lemon juice
- 1 teaspoon sea salt

- 1/2 teaspoon freshly ground black pepper
- Wood embers for roasting (use a hardwood like oak or hickory)

Instructions:

1. Prepare the Sea Urchin:
- Carefully open the sea urchins, extracting the roe (uni) and placing them in a bowl. Be cautious of the spines.
- Rinse the sea urchin roe under cold water to remove any remaining debris.

2. Marinate the Sea Urchin:
- In a small bowl, whisk together the extra-virgin olive oil, fresh lemon juice, sea salt, and black pepper.
- Gently pour the marinade over the sea urchin roe, ensuring they are evenly coated.
- Allow the sea urchin to marinate for 5-10 minutes to absorb the flavors.

3. Prepare the Ember-Roasting Setup:
- Ignite the wood embers in a grill or fireplace, letting them burn down until you have a bed of hot embers.

4. Ember-Roasting:
- Carefully place the sea urchin roe on the hot embers using a heatproof dish or pan.
- Allow the sea urchin to roast for approximately 2-3 minutes, or until the edges begin to char slightly.
- Using tongs, carefully remove the sea urchin from the embers.

5. Serve:
- Arrange the ember-roasted sea urchin on a serving platter.
- Drizzle any remaining marinade over the top for added flavor.
- Serve immediately, allowing your guests to savor the unique combination of sea flavors and smokiness.

Nutrition Information:

Note: Nutritional values are approximate and may vary based on specific ingredients used.
- Calories: 180 per serving
- Protein: 8g
- Fat: 15g
- Carbohydrates: 2g
- Fiber: 0g
- Sugar: 0g
- Sodium: 590mg

Indulge in the extraordinary with this Ember-Roasted Sea Urchin recipe, a testament to the artistry of Asador Etxebarri's culinary mastery.

3. Slow-Cooked Egg with White Truffle

Experience the rustic charm and exquisite flavors of Asador Etxebarri, nestled in the picturesque village of Axpe, Spain. This Slow-Cooked Egg with White Truffle recipe pays homage to the restaurant's dedication to simple, high-quality ingredients and time-honored cooking techniques. Elevate your culinary skills and bring a touch of Basque Country to your table with this indulgent dish that marries the richness of slow-cooked eggs with the earthy aroma of white truffle.

Serving: This recipe serves 2.
Preparation Time: 15 minutes
Ready Time: 1 hour 30 minutes

Ingredients:
- 4 fresh eggs
- 1 tablespoon white truffle oil
- 1 teaspoon white truffle salt
- Freshly ground black pepper, to taste
- Chopped chives, for garnish

Instructions:
1. Preheat the water bath: Fill a sous vide water bath with water and set the temperature to 145°F (63°C).
2. Prepare the eggs: Gently crack each egg into a small bowl, ensuring not to break the yolk. Carefully transfer each egg into a vacuum-sealed bag.
3. Season the eggs: Drizzle each egg with white truffle oil, sprinkle with white truffle salt, and add a dash of freshly ground black pepper.
4. Seal the bags: Vacuum-seal each bag, ensuring a tight seal to prevent water from entering.
5. Cook the eggs: Submerge the sealed bags in the preheated water bath and cook for 1 hour 30 minutes, maintaining a constant temperature.
6. Finish and serve: Carefully remove the eggs from the water bath. Gently crack open each egg onto a plate, letting the silky yolk flow.

Drizzle with additional white truffle oil if desired and sprinkle with chopped chives.

7. Enjoy: Delight in the decadent combination of slow-cooked eggs and the distinctive aroma of white truffle. Serve with crusty bread to mop up every luscious bite.

Nutrition Information (per serving):
- Calories: 220
- Protein: 12g
- Fat: 18g
- Carbohydrates: 1g
- Fiber: 0g
- Sugar: 0g
- Sodium: 800mg

Elevate your culinary repertoire with this Slow-Cooked Egg with White Truffle inspired by the renowned flavors of Asador Etxebarri. A symphony of textures and aromas, this dish is a celebration of simplicity and sophistication.

4. Wood-Grilled Oysters

Experience the rustic charm of Asador Etxebarri, Axpe, Spain, brought to your home with this exquisite recipe for Wood-Grilled Oysters. Inspired by the renowned menu of Asador Etxebarri, this dish captures the essence of traditional Spanish flavors, combining the freshness of oysters with the smoky richness of wood grilling. Elevate your culinary skills and treat your taste buds to a taste of Basque Country's culinary excellence.

Serving: 4 servings
Preparation Time: 15 minutes
Ready Time: 20 minutes

Ingredients:
- 12 fresh oysters, shucked
- 1/2 cup unsalted butter, melted
- 2 cloves garlic, minced
- 1 tablespoon fresh parsley, finely chopped

- 1 teaspoon smoked paprika
- Salt and black pepper to taste
- Lemon wedges for serving

Instructions:
1. Prepare the Grill: Preheat a wood-fired grill to medium-high heat. The distinct smokiness from the wood will impart a unique flavor to the oysters.
2. Prepare the Oysters: Shuck the fresh oysters, being careful to retain as much of the natural juices as possible. Arrange the oysters on a grill-safe tray or plate.
3. Prepare the Garlic Butter Sauce: In a small bowl, mix the melted butter, minced garlic, chopped parsley, smoked paprika, salt, and black pepper. This flavorful butter sauce will enhance the taste of the grilled oysters.
4. Grill the Oysters: Place the shucked oysters directly on the preheated grill. Spoon a generous amount of the garlic butter sauce over each oyster. Close the grill lid and cook for about 5-7 minutes or until the oysters are just cooked through.
5. Serve: Carefully remove the grilled oysters from the grill and arrange them on a serving platter. Drizzle any remaining garlic butter sauce over the top. Serve with lemon wedges on the side.
6. Enjoy: Dive into the tantalizing flavors of these wood-grilled oysters. The smokiness from the wood grill, combined with the savory garlic butter sauce, creates a culinary masterpiece that is sure to delight your palate.

Nutrition Information:
(Per serving)
- Calories: 280
- Total Fat: 22g
- Saturated Fat: 13g
- Cholesterol: 120mg
- Sodium: 420mg
- Total Carbohydrates: 5g
- Dietary Fiber: 1g
- Sugars: 0g
- Protein: 16g

Note: Nutrition information is approximate and may vary based on specific ingredients used.

5. Fire-Grilled Caviar

Elevate your culinary experience with the exquisite flavors of Fire-Grilled Caviar, a dish inspired by the renowned menu of Restaurant Asador Etxebarri in Axpe, Spain. This sophisticated creation captures the essence of the restaurant's commitment to open-fire cooking, infusing the delicate richness of caviar with the smoky nuances of the grill. Prepare to embark on a journey of gastronomic delight as you savor each bite of this luxurious masterpiece.

Serving: Serves 4
Preparation Time: 15 minutes
Ready Time: 20 minutes

Ingredients:
- 4 ounces of high-quality caviar
- 1 tablespoon extra-virgin olive oil
- 1 teaspoon finely chopped chives
- Freshly ground black pepper, to taste
- Sea salt, to taste
- 4 slices of artisanal bread, toasted

Instructions:
1. Prepare the Grill:
- Preheat a charcoal grill or wood-fired grill to medium-high heat.
2. Grill the Bread:
- Place the slices of artisanal bread on the grill grates and toast for 1-2 minutes on each side, or until they develop grill marks and a subtle smokiness. Remove from the grill and set aside.
3. Prepare the Caviar:
- In a small bowl, gently mix the caviar with extra-virgin olive oil, ensuring the caviar is well coated.
4. Assembly:
- Place the grilled bread slices on individual serving plates.
- Spoon a generous amount of the caviar mixture onto each slice.
5. Finishing Touches:
- Sprinkle finely chopped chives over the caviar.

- Grind black pepper and sprinkle sea salt to taste.
6. Serve:
- Present the Fire-Grilled Caviar immediately, allowing guests to indulge in the perfect combination of smokiness and indulgent caviar flavors.

Nutrition Information:
Note: Nutrition values are approximate and may vary based on specific ingredients and serving sizes.
- Calories: 150 per serving
- Total Fat: 7g
- Saturated Fat: 1g
- Trans Fat: 0g
- Cholesterol: 95mg
- Sodium: 300mg
- Total Carbohydrates: 15g
- Dietary Fiber: 1g
- Sugars: 1g
- Protein: 7g

Delight your guests with the unparalleled taste of Fire-Grilled Caviar—a testament to the culinary mastery that defines the menu at Restaurant Asador Etxebarri.

6. Smoked Butter

Discover the rich and irresistible flavor of Smoked Butter, a culinary delight inspired by the renowned menu of Restaurant Asador Etxebarri in Axpe, Spain. Asador Etxebarri is celebrated for its commitment to showcasing the pure essence of quality ingredients, and this smoked butter is no exception. Elevate your dining experience with the smoky nuances of this indulgent condiment, perfect for adding a touch of sophistication to your dishes.

Serving: Makes approximately 1 cup of smoked butter.
Preparation Time: 15 minutes
Ready Time: 3 hours (including smoking time)

Ingredients:
- 1 cup unsalted butter, at room temperature

- 1 tablespoon wood chips (such as oak or hickory), soaked in water for 30 minutes
- 1 teaspoon sea salt

Instructions:

1. Prepare the Smoker:
- If you have a stovetop smoker, set it up according to the manufacturer's instructions. If you don't have a dedicated smoker, you can use a charcoal grill with a smoker box.
- Ensure the wood chips are soaked in water for at least 30 minutes.

2. Soften the Butter:
- Allow the unsalted butter to come to room temperature for optimal blending.

3. Mix in Sea Salt:
- In a mixing bowl, combine the softened butter with the sea salt. Mix thoroughly until the salt is evenly distributed.

4. Shape the Butter:
- Place a sheet of parchment paper on a clean surface. Spoon the butter mixture onto the parchment paper, forming a log or a rectangular shape. Roll the parchment paper around the butter, shaping it into a cylinder.

5. Smoke the Butter:
- Place the soaked wood chips in the smoker or smoker box. Set the butter cylinder on the grate.
- Smoke the butter over low heat for about 2 hours, ensuring a gentle infusion of smoky flavor. Adjust the heat as needed to maintain a consistent low temperature.

6. Chill the Smoked Butter:
- Once smoked, carefully remove the butter from the smoker and refrigerate for at least 1 hour or until firm.

7. Serve and Enjoy:
- Slice the smoked butter as needed and serve with crusty bread, grilled vegetables, or alongside your favorite dishes. The subtle smokiness adds a unique depth to every bite.

Nutrition Information:
(Per tablespoon)
- Calories: 102
- Total Fat: 12g
- Saturated Fat: 7.5g
- Trans Fat: 0g

- Cholesterol: 31mg
- Sodium: 98mg
- Total Carbohydrates: 0g
- Dietary Fiber: 0g
- Sugars: 0g
- Protein: 0.1g

Elevate your culinary repertoire with the exquisite taste of Smoked Butter, a simple yet luxurious addition to your dining experience. Inspired by the mastery of Asador Etxebarri, this recipe brings a touch of Spain to your table.

7. Grilled Razor Clams

Discover the essence of Basque culinary mastery with this recipe inspired by the renowned Asador Etxebarri in Axpe, Spain. Grilled Razor Clams showcase the simplicity and bold flavors that define the restaurant's menu. Savor the taste of the sea with this delectable dish that captures the spirit of Basque gastronomy.

Serving: 4 servings
Preparation Time: 20 minutes
Ready Time: 30 minutes

Ingredients:
- 12 fresh razor clams, cleaned
- 1/4 cup extra-virgin olive oil
- 2 cloves garlic, minced
- 1 tablespoon fresh parsley, chopped
- 1 teaspoon smoked paprika
- Salt and black pepper to taste
- Lemon wedges for serving

Instructions:
1. Prepare the Razor Clams:
- Ensure the razor clams are thoroughly cleaned. Rinse them under cold water and scrub away any sand or debris. Pat them dry with paper towels.
2. Prepare the Grill:
- Preheat a grill or grill pan to medium-high heat.

3. Make the Marinade:
- In a small bowl, combine the olive oil, minced garlic, chopped parsley, smoked paprika, salt, and black pepper. Mix well to create a flavorful marinade.

4. Marinate the Razor Clams:
- Gently brush each razor clam with the prepared marinade, ensuring they are evenly coated.

5. Grill the Razor Clams:
- Place the razor clams on the preheated grill. Grill for 2-3 minutes on each side or until they are opaque and cooked through. Be cautious not to overcook, as razor clams can become tough.

6. Serve:
- Arrange the grilled razor clams on a serving platter. Drizzle any remaining marinade over the top and garnish with additional fresh parsley.

7. Garnish and Enjoy:
- Serve the grilled razor clams with lemon wedges on the side. The citrusy touch enhances the flavors of the dish. Enjoy this exquisite seafood creation inspired by Asador Etxebarri.

Nutrition Information:
(Per Serving)
- Calories: 180
- Protein: 12g
- Carbohydrates: 2g
- Fat: 14g
- Saturated Fat: 2g
- Cholesterol: 45mg
- Sodium: 280mg
- Fiber: 0g

Indulge in the rich tastes of the sea with Grilled Razor Clams, a dish that pays homage to the culinary excellence of Asador Etxebarri in the heart of the Basque Country.

8. Charcoal-Grilled White Asparagus

Experience the rustic flavors of Asador Etxebarri in the comfort of your own home with this exquisite recipe for Charcoal-Grilled White

Asparagus. Inspired by the culinary wonders of Axpe, Spain, this dish captures the essence of the renowned restaurant's dedication to quality ingredients and traditional grilling techniques. Elevate your dining experience with the smoky, charred perfection of white asparagus cooked over charcoal, a true homage to the culinary mastery of Asador Etxebarri.

Serving: Ideal for 4 servings.
Preparation Time: 15 minutes
Ready Time: 25 minutes

Ingredients:
- 1 pound (450g) white asparagus, trimmed
- 2 tablespoons olive oil
- Sea salt, to taste
- Freshly ground black pepper, to taste
- Lemon wedges, for serving

Instructions:
1. Preheat the Grill:
- Prepare a charcoal grill for direct grilling over medium-high heat. Let the charcoal burn until it develops white ash, ensuring a consistent and even heat.
2. Prepare the White Asparagus:
- Trim the tough ends of the white asparagus spears. If the spears are thick, consider peeling them to ensure even cooking.
3. Coat with Olive Oil:
- Drizzle the trimmed asparagus with olive oil, ensuring each spear is lightly coated. Use your hands to toss and evenly distribute the oil.
4. Season with Salt and Pepper:
- Season the asparagus with sea salt and freshly ground black pepper, to taste. The simplicity of these seasonings allows the natural flavors of the asparagus to shine through.
5. Grill the Asparagus:
- Place the seasoned asparagus directly on the preheated grill grates. Grill for 8-10 minutes, turning occasionally, until the asparagus develops a beautiful char and is tender-crisp.
6. Serve Hot:
- Transfer the grilled white asparagus to a serving platter. Squeeze fresh lemon wedges over the asparagus to add a burst of citrusy brightness.

7. Enjoy:
- Serve the Charcoal-Grilled White Asparagus hot, allowing your guests to savor the smoky aroma and robust flavors. This dish makes a perfect appetizer or side to complement a variety of main courses.

Nutrition Information:
Note: Nutritional values are approximate and may vary based on specific ingredients used.
- Calories: 120 per serving
- Fat: 8g
- Saturated Fat: 1g
- Cholesterol: 0mg
- Sodium: 200mg
- Carbohydrates: 10g
- Fiber: 5g
- Sugars: 3g
- Protein: 5g

Elevate your home-cooking experience with this Charcoal-Grilled White Asparagus recipe, inspired by the culinary traditions of Asador Etxebarri. Enjoy the rich flavors and textures that capture the essence of Axpe, Spain's renowned gastronomic scene.

9. Roasted Spring Onions

Transport your taste buds to the rustic charm of Axpe, Spain, with this delectable recipe inspired by the renowned Asador Etxebarri. Roasted Spring Onions showcase the simplicity and elegance of Basque cuisine, highlighting the vibrant flavors of fresh spring produce. This dish perfectly captures the essence of Asador Etxebarri's commitment to exceptional ingredients and expertly executed grilling techniques.

Serving: Ideal for 4 servings.
Preparation Time: 15 minutes
Ready Time: 30 minutes

Ingredients:
- 1 bunch of fresh spring onions
- 2 tablespoons olive oil

- Sea salt, to taste
- Black pepper, freshly ground, to taste
- 1 lemon, cut into wedges (for serving)

Instructions:

1. Preheat the Grill: Prepare your grill for medium-high heat. If using a charcoal grill, allow the coals to become covered with white ash.
2. Clean the Spring Onions: Trim the root ends of the spring onions and remove any loose or discolored outer layers. Rinse them under cold water and pat dry with paper towels.
3. Coat with Olive Oil: Place the spring onions in a bowl and drizzle them with olive oil. Toss until the onions are evenly coated.
4. Season the Onions: Sprinkle the spring onions with sea salt and freshly ground black pepper. Ensure that the seasoning is distributed evenly.
5. Grill the Onions: Lay the spring onions on the preheated grill. Grill for 5-7 minutes, turning occasionally, until they are charred and tender.
6. Serve: Transfer the grilled spring onions to a serving platter. Squeeze fresh lemon juice over them for a burst of citrus flavor. Serve immediately.

Nutrition Information:

Note: Nutrition information is approximate and may vary based on specific ingredients used.
- Calories: 80 per serving
- Total Fat: 7g
- Saturated Fat: 1g
- Cholesterol: 0mg
- Sodium: 200mg
- Total Carbohydrates: 4g
- Dietary Fiber: 2g
- Sugars: 2g
- Protein: 1g

Elevate your culinary experience with these Roasted Spring Onions, a delightful homage to the mastery of Asador Etxebarri's kitchen. The simplicity of this dish allows the natural flavors to shine, creating a memorable dining experience reminiscent of the Basque countryside.

10. Ember-Grilled Palamós Prawns

Embrace the culinary artistry inspired by the renowned Asador Etxebarri in Axpe, Spain, with our Ember-Grilled Palamós Prawns. This dish pays homage to the rustic charm and robust flavors that define the restaurant's menu. The careful selection of fresh Palamós prawns, combined with the primal magic of ember grilling, creates a symphony of taste that transports you to the heart of Basque Country.

Serving: 4 servings
Preparation Time: 15 minutes
Ready Time: 30 minutes

Ingredients:
- 16 large Palamós prawns, peeled and deveined
- 2 tablespoons olive oil
- 1 teaspoon smoked paprika
- 1 teaspoon sea salt
- 1/2 teaspoon black pepper
- 1 lemon, cut into wedges (for serving)

Instructions:
1. Prepare the Ember Grill:
- Ignite the charcoal in your grill, allowing it to burn until covered with white ash. Arrange the hot coals on one side of the grill to create a two-zone cooking area.
2. Marinate the Prawns:
- In a bowl, combine the prawns, olive oil, smoked paprika, sea salt, and black pepper. Toss until the prawns are evenly coated. Let them marinate for 10 minutes, allowing the flavors to meld.
3. Grill the Prawns:
- Place the marinated prawns on the hot side of the grill. Cook for 2-3 minutes on each side, or until they develop a beautiful char and turn opaque. Be attentive to prevent overcooking.
4. Rest and Serve:
- Remove the prawns from the grill and let them rest for a couple of minutes. This allows the juices to redistribute, ensuring a succulent bite. Serve the ember-grilled Palamós prawns with lemon wedges on the side.

Nutrition Information:

Note: Nutritional values are approximate and may vary based on specific ingredients used.
- Calories: 180 per serving
- Protein: 20g
- Fat: 9g
- Carbohydrates: 2g
- Fiber: 1g
- Sugar: 0g
- Cholesterol: 180mg
- Sodium: 600mg

Elevate your culinary experience with the Ember-Grilled Palamós Prawns, a dish that captures the essence of Asador Etxebarri's distinctive approach to traditional Basque cuisine.

11. Grilled Squid with Ink Sauce

Embark on a culinary journey inspired by the rustic charm and exquisite flavors of Asador Etxebarri in Axpe, Spain. Renowned for its mastery in grilling, the restaurant elevates the art of barbecue with dishes like Grilled Squid with Ink Sauce. This recipe captures the essence of Asador Etxebarri's inventive menu, where simplicity meets sophistication. Prepare to indulge in the tantalizing flavors of the sea with this sumptuous grilled squid dish, adorned with a rich and velvety ink sauce.

Serving: 4 servings
Preparation Time: 15 minutes
Ready Time: 30 minutes

Ingredients:
- 4 whole squids, cleaned and tentacles reserved
- 2 tablespoons olive oil
- Salt and black pepper to taste
- For the Ink Sauce:
- 1/4 cup squid ink (available in specialty stores)
- 2 tablespoons olive oil
- 2 cloves garlic, minced
- 1/2 cup dry white wine
- Salt and black pepper to taste

- Fresh parsley, chopped, for garnish

Instructions:
1. Preheat the grill to medium-high heat.
2. Rinse the squid under cold water and pat them dry with paper towels. Score the squid bodies in a crisscross pattern without cutting through.
3. In a bowl, toss the squid and tentacles with olive oil, salt, and black pepper, ensuring they are well coated.
4. Place the squid on the preheated grill and cook for about 2-3 minutes per side until they develop a beautiful char and are just cooked through. Add the tentacles during the last minute of grilling.
5. For the Ink Sauce: In a saucepan, heat olive oil over medium heat. Add minced garlic and sauté until fragrant.
6. Pour in the white wine and simmer for 2 minutes to allow the alcohol to cook off. Stir in the squid ink, salt, and black pepper. Simmer for an additional 5 minutes, allowing the flavors to meld.
7. Drizzle the ink sauce over the grilled squid and garnish with fresh chopped parsley.
8. Serve the Grilled Squid with Ink Sauce immediately, accompanied by crusty bread to savor every drop of the flavorful sauce.

Nutrition Information:
Note: Nutritional values are approximate and may vary based on specific ingredients used.
- Calories: 250 per serving
- Protein: 20g
- Fat: 12g
- Carbohydrates: 8g
- Fiber: 1g
- Sugars: 0g
- Sodium: 400mg

Elevate your dining experience with this Grilled Squid with Ink Sauce, a homage to the culinary brilliance of Asador Etxebarri in the heart of Axpe, Spain.

12. Grilled Baby Leeks

Elevate your culinary experience with the exquisite flavor of Grilled Baby Leeks inspired by the renowned Asador Etxebarri in Axpe, Spain. This simple yet sophisticated dish captures the essence of the restaurant's dedication to highlighting the natural, smoky essence of ingredients. The tender baby leeks, kissed by the flames, offer a delightful harmony of charred sweetness, making this dish a testament to the artistry of Basque cuisine.

Serving: Ideal for 4 servings.
Preparation Time: 15 minutes
Ready Time: 30 minutes

Ingredients:
- 12 baby leeks, cleaned and trimmed
- 2 tablespoons olive oil
- Sea salt, to taste
- Freshly ground black pepper, to taste
- Lemon wedges, for serving

Instructions:
1. Preheat the Grill:
- Prepare your grill for direct grilling over medium-high heat.
2. Prepare the Baby Leeks:
- Trim the roots from the baby leeks and remove any tough outer leaves. Rinse them under cold water to remove any dirt or sand.
3. Brush with Olive Oil:
- In a bowl, toss the baby leeks with olive oil until they are well-coated. This will enhance their flavor and prevent them from sticking to the grill.
4. Season:
- Season the leeks with sea salt and freshly ground black pepper. Adjust according to your taste preferences.
5. Grill the Baby Leeks:
- Place the seasoned baby leeks directly on the preheated grill grates. Grill for about 3-5 minutes per side or until they are tender and have a nice char.
6. Check for Doneness:
- Use a fork to check for tenderness. The leeks should be soft but not mushy.
7. Serve:

- Transfer the grilled baby leeks to a serving platter. Squeeze fresh lemon juice over them for a burst of citrusy brightness.

8. Enjoy:
- Serve these Grilled Baby Leeks as a delightful side dish or appetizer, showcasing the natural flavors enhanced by the smoky embrace of the grill.

Nutrition Information:
- *Note: Nutritional values may vary based on specific ingredients used and portion sizes.*
- Calories per serving: XX
- Total Fat: XXg
- Saturated Fat: XXg
- Cholesterol: XXmg
- Sodium: XXmg
- Total Carbohydrates: XXg
- Dietary Fiber: XXg
- Sugars: XXg
- Protein: XXg

Elevate your culinary skills with this simple yet sophisticated Grilled Baby Leeks recipe inspired by the culinary excellence of Asador Etxebarri. Enjoy the smoky, charred goodness in every bite!

13. Ember-Cooked Scarlet Shrimp

Experience the rustic charm and unparalleled flavors of Asador Etxebarri, Axpe, Spain, right in your own kitchen with our Ember-Cooked Scarlet Shrimp recipe. Inspired by the renowned restaurant's dedication to open-flame cooking, this dish captures the essence of simplicity and perfection. Let the smoky embrace of embers elevate your culinary journey with every succulent bite.

Serving: Serves 4
Preparation Time: 15 minutes
Ready Time: 30 minutes

Ingredients:
- 1 pound Scarlet Shrimp, peeled and deveined

- 2 tablespoons olive oil
- 1 teaspoon smoked paprika
- 1/2 teaspoon sea salt
- 1/4 teaspoon freshly ground black pepper
- 1 lemon, cut into wedges
- Fresh parsley, chopped, for garnish

Instructions:
1. Prepare the Ember Bed:
- Heat a charcoal grill or fire pit until the embers are glowing with a gentle flame.
2. Marinate the Shrimp:
- In a bowl, toss the Scarlet Shrimp with olive oil, smoked paprika, sea salt, and black pepper. Ensure the shrimp are evenly coated.
3. Skewer the Shrimp:
- Thread the marinated shrimp onto skewers, ensuring they are well spaced for even cooking.
4. Ember-Cooking:
- Place the shrimp skewers directly on the ember bed. Cook for approximately 2-3 minutes per side or until the shrimp are opaque and have a slight char.
5. Serve:
- Remove the shrimp skewers from the embers and transfer them to a serving platter. Squeeze fresh lemon juice over the shrimp and garnish with chopped parsley.
6. Enjoy:
- Serve the Ember-Cooked Scarlet Shrimp immediately, allowing your guests to savor the smoky aroma and robust flavors. Pair with a side of crusty bread or a simple salad for a complete meal.

Nutrition Information:
- *Note: Nutritional values may vary depending on specific ingredients and portion sizes.*
- Calories per serving: XXX
- Protein: XXXg
- Fat: XXXg
- Carbohydrates: XXXg
- Fiber: XXXg
- Sugar: XXXg
- Sodium: XXXmg

Embrace the warmth of the embers and the essence of Asador Etxebarri with this Ember-Cooked Scarlet Shrimp recipe—a culinary journey that celebrates the art of open-flame cooking.

14. Oak-Grilled Artichokes

Delight your palate with the smoky goodness of Oak-Grilled Artichokes, a culinary masterpiece inspired by the renowned Asador Etxebarri in Axpe, Spain. This dish captures the essence of open-fire cooking, infusing the artichokes with a rich, charred flavor that will transport you to the rustic charm of Spanish countryside dining. Simple yet sophisticated, this recipe is a testament to the art of grilling perfected by Asador Etxebarri.

Serving: 4 servings
Preparation Time: 15 minutes
Ready Time: 45 minutes

Ingredients:
- 8 large artichokes, cleaned and trimmed
- 1/4 cup extra-virgin olive oil
- 3 cloves garlic, minced
- 1 teaspoon smoked paprika
- Salt and black pepper, to taste
- Fresh lemon wedges, for garnish

Instructions:
1. Prepare the Artichokes:
- Trim the tough outer leaves of the artichokes, leaving only the tender inner leaves.
- Cut off the top inch of each artichoke, and trim the stem, leaving about 1 inch.
- Use a knife or kitchen shears to trim the pointed tips of the remaining leaves.
- Rub the cut surfaces with lemon to prevent browning.
2. Preheat the Grill:
- Prepare a charcoal or oak grill for medium-high heat.
3. Garlic Infused Olive Oil:

- In a small saucepan, heat the olive oil over medium heat.
- Add minced garlic and cook until fragrant, about 1-2 minutes.
- Stir in smoked paprika, and season with salt and black pepper.
- Remove from heat and set aside.

4. Grill the Artichokes:
- Place the prepared artichokes on the preheated grill.
- Grill for 15-20 minutes, turning occasionally, until the leaves are charred and the artichokes are tender.
- Baste the artichokes with the garlic-infused olive oil mixture during grilling.

5. Serve:
- Arrange the grilled artichokes on a serving platter.
- Drizzle with any remaining garlic-infused olive oil.
- Serve with fresh lemon wedges for a burst of citrusy flavor.

Nutrition Information:
(Per serving)
- Calories: 180
- Total Fat: 12g
- Saturated Fat: 2g
- Cholesterol: 0mg
- Sodium: 120mg
- Total Carbohydrates: 18g
- Dietary Fiber: 8g
- Sugars: 2g
- Protein: 5g

Elevate your dining experience with these Oak-Grilled Artichokes, a testament to the culinary mastery of Asador Etxebarri. Enjoy the smoky, charred perfection of this simple yet elegant dish that brings the flavors of the Spanish countryside to your table.

15. Grilled Cuttlefish

Grilled cuttlefish is a delightful dish that captures the essence of Asador Etxebarri's renowned menu. This recipe celebrates the freshness of seafood and the flavors imparted by the grill, creating a savory, smoky delight. With simple yet high-quality ingredients, this dish showcases the excellence of Spanish cuisine.

Serving: Serves: 4
Preparation Time: Preparation: 15 minutes
Ready Time: Ready in: 30 minutes

Ingredients:
- 2 large cuttlefish, cleaned and sliced into medium pieces
- 4 tablespoons olive oil
- 2 cloves garlic, minced
- 1 tablespoon fresh parsley, finely chopped
- Salt and pepper to taste
- Lemon wedges for garnish

Instructions:
1. Prepare the Cuttlefish: Rinse the cuttlefish under cold water and pat dry with paper towels. Slice it into medium-sized pieces.
2. Marinate the Cuttlefish: In a bowl, combine the olive oil, minced garlic, chopped parsley, salt, and pepper. Add the cuttlefish pieces to the mixture, ensuring they are well-coated. Allow it to marinate for 10 minutes.
3. Preheat the Grill: Heat a grill or grill pan over medium-high heat. Make sure the grill grates are clean and lightly oiled to prevent sticking.
4. Grill the Cuttlefish: Place the marinated cuttlefish pieces on the grill and cook for 2-3 minutes per side, or until they develop a lightly charred exterior and are cooked through. Be cautious not to overcook to maintain tenderness.
5. Serve: Once grilled, transfer the cuttlefish to a serving platter. Garnish with fresh parsley and lemon wedges for a burst of citrus flavor.

Nutrition Information (per serving):
- Calories: Approximately 200 kcal
- Protein: 20g
- Carbohydrates: 2g
- Fat: 12g
- Fiber: 0.5g

Note: Nutritional values are approximate and may vary based on portion sizes and specific ingredients used.

Enjoy this grilled cuttlefish dish hot off the grill, savoring the smoky aroma and tender texture, reminiscent of the exceptional flavors found at Asador Etxebarri.

16. Wood-Fired Piquillos Peppers

The wood-fired piquillos peppers draw inspiration from the culinary legacy of Asador Etxebarri in Axpe, Spain. This dish encapsulates the essence of simplicity and authenticity, allowing the natural flavors of high-quality ingredients to shine through the smoky essence of the wood-fired cooking technique.

Serving: 4 servings
Preparation time: 15 minutes
Ready time: 45 minutes

Ingredients:
- 12 whole piquillo peppers, drained and patted dry
- 1 cup goat cheese, softened
- 2 cloves garlic, minced
- 1 tablespoon fresh parsley, finely chopped
- Salt and pepper to taste
- Extra-virgin olive oil

Instructions:
1. Prepare the Filling:
- In a bowl, combine the softened goat cheese, minced garlic, chopped parsley, salt, and pepper. Mix thoroughly to create a smooth, well-incorporated filling.
2. Fill the Piquillos Peppers:
- Carefully open each piquillo pepper and gently stuff them with the prepared goat cheese mixture. Ensure they are evenly filled without overstuffing.
3. Fire Up the Grill:
- Preheat a wood-fired grill or oven to medium-high heat. Ensure the grates are clean and lightly oiled to prevent sticking.
4. Grill the Stuffed Peppers:
- Brush the stuffed piquillo peppers lightly with olive oil. Place them directly onto the grill grates or on a grill-safe tray. Cook for about 5-7 minutes, turning occasionally, until the peppers develop a slight char and the cheese begins to melt.

5. Serve and Enjoy:
- Remove the wood-fired piquillos peppers from the grill and transfer them to a serving platter. Garnish with a drizzle of high-quality extra-virgin olive oil and additional chopped parsley if desired. Serve hot as an appetizer or part of a tapas spread.

Nutrition Information (per serving):
- Calories: 180
- Total Fat: 12g
- Saturated Fat: 6g
- Cholesterol: 25mg
- Sodium: 320mg
- Total Carbohydrate: 10g
- Dietary Fiber: 2g
- Sugars: 3g
- Protein: 8g

Adjust the serving size and ingredients as needed to accommodate dietary preferences or requirements. Enjoy the smoky, savory flavors of these wood-fired piquillos peppers, a testament to the rustic elegance of Basque cuisine.

17. Ember-Grilled Scallops

Inspired by the exceptional menu of the renowned Asador Etxebarri in Axpe, Spain, these Ember-Grilled Scallops encapsulate the essence of exquisite Basque cuisine. The simple yet sophisticated preparation allows the natural flavors of the scallops to shine, enhanced by the smoky essence of ember grilling.

Serving: Serves: 4
Serving Size: 3 scallops per person
Preparation time: 20 minutes
Ready time: 30 minutes

Ingredients:
- 12 large, fresh scallops, cleaned and patted dry
- Sea salt (preferably flaky or coarse)
- Freshly ground black pepper

- High-quality olive oil

Instructions:
1. Prepare a charcoal grill for direct grilling over high heat. Let the coals burn until covered with a thin layer of ash, ensuring a medium-high heat.
2. While the grill heats, season both sides of the scallops generously with sea salt and freshly ground black pepper.
3. Drizzle a touch of olive oil over the scallops, just enough to lightly coat them.
4. Place the seasoned scallops directly onto the grill grates over the high heat. Cook for approximately 1.5 to 2 minutes per side. The scallops should develop a beautiful sear and grill marks while remaining tender inside.
5. Carefully remove the scallops from the grill and transfer them to a serving platter.
6. Drizzle a touch more olive oil over the grilled scallops before serving.

Nutrition Information (per serving):
- Calories: 150
- Total Fat: 6g
- Saturated Fat: 1g
- Cholesterol: 35mg
- Sodium: 500mg
- Total Carbohydrate: 2g
- Protein: 20g

Enjoy these ember-grilled scallops as a delightful appetizer or a flavorful addition to a seafood-inspired meal. The simplicity of the preparation allows the quality of the scallops to take center stage, offering a taste of the exquisite flavors celebrated at Asador Etxebarri.

18. Grilled Octopus

Inspired by the culinary excellence of Asador Etxebarri in Axpe, Spain, this Grilled Octopus recipe captures the essence of traditional Basque cuisine with a modern twist. Known for their commitment to using top-quality, locally sourced ingredients, Asador Etxebarri elevates the experience of grilled octopus to new heights. This dish is a celebration of the rich flavors and artisanal techniques that define the restaurant's menu.

Serving: 4 servings
Preparation Time: 20 minutes
Ready Time: 1 hour and 30 minutes

Ingredients:
- 2 pounds fresh octopus, cleaned
- 1/4 cup extra virgin olive oil
- 2 cloves garlic, minced
- 1 teaspoon smoked paprika
- 1 teaspoon sea salt
- 1/2 teaspoon black pepper
- Zest of 1 lemon
- Juice of 1 lemon
- Fresh parsley, chopped (for garnish)

Instructions:
1. Preheat the Grill:
- Preheat a grill to medium-high heat. Make sure the grates are clean and well-oiled.
2. Prepare the Octopus:
- Rinse the octopus under cold water and pat it dry with paper towels.
- If the octopus has a beak, remove it and discard. Cut the tentacles apart if they are still attached.
3. Marinate the Octopus:
- In a bowl, whisk together the olive oil, minced garlic, smoked paprika, sea salt, black pepper, lemon zest, and lemon juice to create a marinade.
- Place the octopus in a shallow dish and coat it evenly with the marinade. Allow it to marinate for at least 1 hour in the refrigerator, turning it occasionally.
4. Grill the Octopus:
- Remove the octopus from the refrigerator and let it come to room temperature for about 15 minutes.
- Grill the octopus for approximately 10-15 minutes, turning occasionally, until it is charred on the outside and tender on the inside.
5. Serve:
- Transfer the grilled octopus to a serving platter, sprinkle with fresh parsley, and drizzle with a bit of extra olive oil.

- Serve immediately, either as a stand-alone dish or alongside your favorite side dishes.

Nutrition Information:
- *Note: Nutritional values are approximate and may vary based on specific ingredients and portion sizes.*
- Calories: 250 per serving
- Protein: 30g
- Fat: 14g
- Carbohydrates: 2g
- Fiber: 1g
- Sugar: 0g
- Sodium: 600mg

Embrace the bold flavors of the Basque region with this Grilled Octopus recipe, paying homage to the culinary mastery of Asador Etxebarri. Enjoy the delightful combination of smoky, tender octopus infused with the richness of Spanish spices and the brightness of fresh lemon.

19. Fire-Roasted Red Prawns

Indulge your senses in the smoky allure of Asador Etxebarri, Axpe, Spain, with our Fire-Roasted Red Prawns recipe. Inspired by the culinary magic of this renowned restaurant, these prawns are a celebration of simplicity and the art of open-fire cooking. The dish captures the essence of Asador Etxebarri's commitment to using premium, locally-sourced ingredients to create unforgettable flavors. Fire up your grill and embark on a gastronomic journey that pays homage to the rich culinary traditions of Spain.

Serving: 4 servings
Preparation Time: 15 minutes
Ready Time: 30 minutes

Ingredients:
- 16 large red prawns, peeled and deveined
- 2 tablespoons extra virgin olive oil
- 2 cloves garlic, minced
- 1 teaspoon smoked paprika

- 1 teaspoon sea salt
- 1/2 teaspoon freshly ground black pepper
- 1 lemon, cut into wedges
- Fresh parsley, chopped (for garnish)

Instructions:
1. Prepare the Grill:
- Preheat a grill to high heat. Ensure the grates are clean and well-oiled to prevent sticking.
2. Marinate the Prawns:
- In a bowl, combine the peeled and deveined prawns with olive oil, minced garlic, smoked paprika, sea salt, and black pepper. Toss the prawns until evenly coated in the marinade.
3. Skewer the Prawns:
- Thread the marinated prawns onto skewers, ensuring they are evenly spaced.
4. Grill the Prawns:
- Place the skewers on the preheated grill and cook for 2-3 minutes per side or until the prawns are opaque and have a slight char from the open flame.
5. Serve:
- Remove the prawns from the grill and transfer them to a serving platter. Squeeze fresh lemon juice over the top and sprinkle with chopped fresh parsley.
6. Garnish and Enjoy:
- Garnish with additional lemon wedges and parsley. Serve the Fire-Roasted Red Prawns hot, allowing your guests to savor the smoky, succulent flavors.

Nutrition Information:
Note: Nutritional values are approximate and may vary based on specific ingredients used.
- Calories: 220 per serving
- Protein: 20g
- Fat: 14g
- Carbohydrates: 3g
- Fiber: 1g
- Sugar: 0g
- Cholesterol: 180mg
- Sodium: 680mg

Immerse yourself in the authenticity of Spanish cuisine with these Fire-Roasted Red Prawns – a testament to the culinary excellence that defines Asador Etxebarri.

20. Whole Grilled Lobster

Indulge in the exquisite flavors of Asador Etxebarri, Axpe, Spain, with this Whole Grilled Lobster recipe that captures the essence of their renowned culinary expertise. This dish exemplifies the restaurant's dedication to simplicity and quality ingredients, allowing the natural flavors of the lobster to shine. Prepare to elevate your dining experience with this sophisticated yet straightforward recipe that celebrates the essence of Spanish gastronomy.

Serving: 4 servings
Preparation Time: 15 minutes
Ready Time: 30 minutes

Ingredients:
- 4 whole lobsters (approximately 1.5 pounds each)
- 1/2 cup extra-virgin olive oil
- 4 cloves garlic, minced
- 2 tablespoons fresh parsley, chopped
- 1 teaspoon smoked paprika
- Salt and black pepper to taste
- Lemon wedges for serving

Instructions:
1. Preheat the Grill:
- Prepare a grill for medium-high heat. If using a charcoal grill, wait until the coals are covered with white ash. For a gas grill, preheat to medium-high.
2. Prepare the Lobsters:
- Rinse the lobsters under cold water and pat them dry with paper towels.
- Using a sharp knife, carefully split each lobster in half lengthwise. Remove the digestive tract (dark vein) if present.
3. Make the Marinade:

- In a small bowl, combine the olive oil, minced garlic, chopped parsley, smoked paprika, salt, and black pepper. Mix well to create a flavorful marinade.

4. Marinate the Lobsters:
- Brush the lobster halves generously with the prepared marinade, ensuring each piece is well-coated.

5. Grill the Lobsters:
- Place the lobster halves on the preheated grill, cut side down. Cook for about 6-8 minutes, basting with the marinade occasionally, until the lobster meat is opaque and lightly charred.

6. Serve:
- Transfer the grilled lobsters to a serving platter. Drizzle any remaining marinade over the top and garnish with fresh parsley.
- Serve hot with lemon wedges on the side.

Nutrition Information:
(Per Serving)
- Calories: 350
- Protein: 30g
- Fat: 22g
- Carbohydrates: 2g
- Fiber: 0g
- Sugars: 0g
- Cholesterol: 150mg
- Sodium: 450mg

Elevate your dining experience with this Whole Grilled Lobster inspired by the culinary treasures of Asador Etxebarri. This dish encapsulates the spirit of Spanish cuisine, celebrating the natural flavors of the sea in a harmonious blend of simplicity and sophistication.

21. Ember-Grilled Langoustines

Experience the rustic charm of Asador Etxebarri, Axpe, Spain, as you embark on a culinary journey inspired by their renowned menu. One dish that captures the essence of open-fire cooking is the Ember-Grilled Langoustines. Delight in the smoky flavors and succulent tenderness of langoustines kissed by the flames. This recipe brings the soulful simplicity of Spanish grilling to your home kitchen.

Serving: 4 servings
Preparation Time: 15 minutes
Ready Time: 30 minutes

Ingredients:
- 12 langoustines, cleaned and deveined
- 3 tablespoons olive oil
- 2 cloves garlic, minced
- 1 teaspoon smoked paprika
- Salt and black pepper to taste
- Fresh parsley, chopped (for garnish)
- Lemon wedges (for serving)

Instructions:
1. Prepare the langoustines:
- Using kitchen shears, cut through the top shell of each langoustine, exposing the meat.
- Gently butterfly the langoustines by spreading them open slightly to allow for even cooking.
2. Marinate the langoustines:
- In a bowl, combine olive oil, minced garlic, smoked paprika, salt, and black pepper.
- Brush the langoustines with the marinade, ensuring they are well coated. Allow them to marinate for at least 10 minutes.
3. Preheat the grill:
- Prepare a charcoal or wood-fired grill and let the embers burn down until you have a bed of hot, glowing coals.
4. Grill the langoustines:
- Place the langoustines on the grill, shell side down, over the hot embers.
- Grill for 2-3 minutes on each side or until the shells are charred, and the meat is opaque and cooked through.
5. Serve:
- Arrange the grilled langoustines on a serving platter.
- Garnish with chopped fresh parsley and serve with lemon wedges on the side.

Nutrition Information:

- *Note: Nutritional values are approximate and may vary based on specific ingredients used.*
- Calories: 180 per serving
- Protein: 20g
- Fat: 10g
- Carbohydrates: 2g
- Fiber: 1g
- Sugar: 0g
- Sodium: 350mg

Enjoy the Ember-Grilled Langoustines as a testament to the rich culinary traditions of Asador Etxebarri, bringing the essence of Spanish grilling to your table.

22. Oak-Smoked Foie Gras

Indulge your senses in the sublime world of Asador Etxebarri with this exquisite Oak-Smoked Foie Gras recipe. Inspired by the culinary mastery of this renowned restaurant in Axpe, Spain, this dish elevates the rich and buttery flavors of foie gras with the nuanced essence of oak smoke. A symphony of textures and tastes awaits, making it a perfect choice for those seeking a sophisticated and memorable dining experience.

Serving: 4 servings
Preparation Time: 20 minutes
Ready Time: 2 hours (including chilling time)

Ingredients:
- 4 slices of high-quality foie gras (approximately 200g each)
- Oak wood chips, soaked in water for 30 minutes
- Sea salt, to taste
- Freshly ground black pepper, to taste
- Baguette slices, lightly toasted (optional, for serving)

Instructions:
1. Prepare the Foie Gras:
- Carefully trim any excess veins or membranes from the foie gras slices.
- Season each slice generously with sea salt and freshly ground black pepper.

2. Oak Smoking:
- Preheat your smoker or charcoal grill to a low heat (around 200°F/93°C).
- Sprinkle the soaked oak wood chips over the hot coals or smoker box.
- Place the foie gras slices on the grate, ensuring they are not directly over the heat source.
- Close the lid and smoke the foie gras for about 10-15 minutes, allowing it to absorb the delicate oak flavor. Adjust the time based on your desired level of smokiness.

3. Chill and Rest:
- Remove the foie gras from the smoker and let it cool to room temperature.
- Refrigerate the foie gras for at least 1-2 hours to allow the flavors to meld and the texture to firm up.

4. Serve:
- Before serving, allow the foie gras to come to a cool room temperature.
- Optionally, serve the smoked foie gras with lightly toasted baguette slices to complement its richness.

Nutrition Information:
- *(Note: Nutritional values may vary based on the specific product and preparation method.)*
- Calories per serving: XXX
- Protein: XXXg
- Fat: XXXg
- Carbohydrates: XXXg
- Fiber: XXXg
- Sugar: XXXg
- Sodium: XXXmg

Indulge in the refined flavors of this Oak-Smoked Foie Gras, a culinary journey that pays homage to the mastery of Asador Etxebarri. Immerse yourself in the enchanting blend of oak-infused elegance, as each bite takes you on a sensory adventure inspired by the heart of Spain.

23. Grilled Bonito Fish

Experience the essence of Asador Etxebarri, Axpe, Spain, in your own kitchen with this delightful recipe for Grilled Bonito Fish. Inspired by the restaurant's dedication to showcasing the natural flavors of quality ingredients, this dish brings the smoky charm of the traditional Basque grill to your table.

Serving: 4 servings
Preparation Time: 15 minutes
Ready Time: 30 minutes

Ingredients:
- 4 bonito fish fillets (about 6 ounces each)
- 2 tablespoons olive oil
- 1 teaspoon sea salt
- 1/2 teaspoon black pepper
- 2 cloves garlic, minced
- 1 lemon, sliced
- Fresh parsley, chopped (for garnish)

Instructions:
1. Prepare the Grill:
Preheat your grill to medium-high heat, ensuring the grates are clean and lightly oiled.
2. Season the Bonito:
Pat the bonito fillets dry with paper towels. Brush both sides of each fillet with olive oil and season with sea salt and black pepper.
3. Grill the Bonito:
Place the bonito fillets on the preheated grill. Grill for 3-4 minutes on each side or until the fish is opaque and easily flakes with a fork. Be cautious not to overcook, as bonito has a delicate texture.
4. Infuse with Garlic:
In the last minute of grilling, sprinkle minced garlic over the fillets. Allow the garlic to infuse its flavor into the fish, turning once to ensure even distribution.
5. Serve with Lemon:
Transfer the grilled bonito to a serving platter. Squeeze fresh lemon juice over the fillets and garnish with lemon slices.
6. Garnish and Serve:
Sprinkle chopped fresh parsley over the grilled bonito for a burst of color and additional freshness. Serve immediately, allowing your guests to savor the smoky aroma and rich flavors.

Nutrition Information:
Note: Nutritional values are approximate and may vary based on specific ingredients used.
- Calories: 220 per serving
- Protein: 25g
- Fat: 12g
- Carbohydrates: 2g
- Fiber: 1g
- Sugar: 0g

Elevate your dining experience with the Grilled Bonito Fish inspired by the culinary excellence of Asador Etxebarri. This dish captures the essence of Spanish grilling, delivering a delightful harmony of flavors that will transport you to the heart of Axpe, Spain.

24. Ember-Cooked Sardines

Elevate your culinary experience with the smoky essence of Ember-Cooked Sardines, a dish inspired by the exquisite menu of Restaurant Asador Etxebarri in Axpe, Spain. This recipe captures the essence of traditional Basque cuisine, infusing the rich flavors of the open flame into tender sardines. Immerse yourself in the art of ember cooking, where simplicity meets sophistication, and every bite tells a story of Spanish culinary mastery.

Serving: Ideal for sharing, this recipe serves 4.
Preparation Time: 15 minutes
Ready Time: 30 minutes

Ingredients:
- 12 fresh sardines, gutted and cleaned
- 1/4 cup extra-virgin olive oil
- 2 cloves garlic, minced
- 1 tablespoon fresh parsley, chopped
- Salt and black pepper to taste
- Lemon wedges for garnish

Instructions:
1. Prepare the Ember Bed:

- Start a hardwood fire, allowing it to burn down until you have a bed of hot embers.

2. Clean and Season the Sardines:
- Rinse the sardines under cold water and pat them dry with paper towels.
- In a bowl, mix olive oil, minced garlic, chopped parsley, salt, and black pepper.
- Coat the sardines with this mixture, ensuring they are well-seasoned.

3. Cooking Over Embers:
- Place the sardines directly onto the hot embers, arranging them in a single layer.
- Cook for about 3-4 minutes on each side, or until the skin is crispy and the flesh is cooked through.
- Use a long spatula to carefully flip the sardines.

4. Serve:
- Remove the sardines from the embers and arrange them on a serving platter.
- Drizzle with extra olive oil and sprinkle with additional chopped parsley.
- Serve hot with lemon wedges on the side.

Nutrition Information:
Note: Nutritional values are approximate and may vary based on specific ingredients used.
- Calories: 220 per serving
- Protein: 25g
- Fat: 12g
- Carbohydrates: 1g
- Fiber: 0.5g
- Sugar: 0g
- Sodium: 350mg

Embrace the essence of Asador Etxebarri in your own kitchen with Ember-Cooked Sardines—a dish that brings the flavors of Spain's culinary gem to your table. Enjoy the simplicity and authenticity of Basque cuisine with each mouthwatering bite.

25. Grilled Mackerel with Green Pepper

Indulge in the rustic charm of Spanish cuisine with this delectable recipe inspired by the renowned Asador Etxebarri in Axpe, Spain. Grilled Mackerel with Green Pepper captures the essence of the restaurant's commitment to using high-quality, locally sourced ingredients to create a symphony of flavors. The dish brings together the bold taste of mackerel and the vibrant kick of green pepper, offering a culinary journey that celebrates simplicity and authenticity.

Serving: 4 servings
Preparation Time: 15 minutes
Ready Time: 30 minutes

Ingredients:
- 4 fresh mackerel fillets
- 2 large green peppers, sliced
- 3 tablespoons olive oil
- 2 cloves garlic, minced
- 1 teaspoon smoked paprika
- Salt and pepper to taste
- Lemon wedges for garnish

Instructions:
1. Prepare the Mackerel:
- Clean and pat dry the mackerel fillets.
- Season the fillets with salt, pepper, and smoked paprika, ensuring an even coating.
2. Grill the Mackerel:
- Preheat the grill to medium-high heat.
- Brush the mackerel fillets with olive oil to prevent sticking.
- Grill the fillets for 3-4 minutes on each side, or until the flesh is opaque and easily flakes with a fork.
3. Sauté the Green Peppers:
- In a skillet, heat 2 tablespoons of olive oil over medium heat.
- Add the sliced green peppers and minced garlic, sautéing until the peppers are tender but still vibrant.
4. Combine and Serve:
- Arrange the grilled mackerel fillets on a serving platter.
- Spoon the sautéed green peppers over the top.
- Drizzle with the remaining olive oil and garnish with lemon wedges.

Nutrition Information:
- *Note: Nutrition information is per serving.*
- Calories: 280
- Protein: 22g
- Carbohydrates: 5g
- Fat: 19g
- Saturated Fat: 3g
- Cholesterol: 60mg
- Sodium: 80mg
- Fiber: 2g
- Sugar: 2g

Enjoy this Grilled Mackerel with Green Pepper dish as a testament to the Asador Etxebarri's culinary expertise, bringing a taste of Spain to your own kitchen. Buen provecho!

26. Wood-Grilled Turbot

Delight your senses with the exquisite flavors of Asador Etxebarri, a renowned restaurant nestled in the picturesque village of Axpe, Spain. Known for its commitment to traditional Basque cuisine and wood-fired cooking techniques, Asador Etxebarri has inspired this tantalizing recipe for Wood-Grilled Turbot. The wood-grilling method imparts a smoky essence to the delicate turbot, creating a culinary masterpiece that transports you to the heart of Spanish gastronomy.

Serving: This Wood-Grilled Turbot is perfect for an intimate dinner for two or a special gathering of friends and family. Pair it with a crisp white wine or a light-bodied Spanish red to complement the smoky notes of the dish.

Preparation Time: 20 minutes
Ready Time: 45 minutes

Ingredients:
- 2 fresh turbot fillets (6-8 ounces each)
- 2 tablespoons olive oil
- 1 teaspoon sea salt
- 1/2 teaspoon freshly ground black pepper
- 1 lemon, thinly sliced for garnish

- Fresh parsley, chopped for garnish
- Wood chips for grilling (preferably oak or cherry)

Instructions:
1. Preheat your wood grill to medium-high heat, ensuring the flames have subsided, and the coals are covered with white ash.
2. Pat the turbot fillets dry with paper towels. Brush both sides with olive oil, ensuring they are well-coated.
3. Season the fillets with sea salt and freshly ground black pepper, evenly distributing the seasoning on both sides.
4. Soak the wood chips in water for about 15 minutes to prevent them from burning too quickly on the grill.
5. Once the wood chips are ready, scatter them over the hot coals to create a smoky environment.
6. Carefully place the turbot fillets on the preheated grill. Grill for approximately 4-5 minutes per side, or until the fish easily flakes with a fork and has a beautiful golden-brown color.
7. While grilling, add a few lemon slices to the grill for a subtle citrus infusion.
8. Once the turbot is cooked, remove it from the grill and let it rest for a few minutes.
9. Garnish the wood-grilled turbot with fresh lemon slices and chopped parsley before serving.

Nutrition Information:
(Per Serving)
- Calories: 300
- Protein: 35g
- Fat: 17g
- Carbohydrates: 2g
- Fiber: 1g
- Sugar: 0g
- Sodium: 650mg

Savor the essence of Asador Etxebarri with this Wood-Grilled Turbot recipe, celebrating the rich culinary heritage of Axpe, Spain.

27. Ember-Roasted Monkfish

Experience the rustic charm and culinary mastery of Asador Etxebarri, nestled in the heart of Axpe, Spain. Our cookbook, inspired by the restaurant's menu, brings you a symphony of flavors, and one standout dish is the Ember-Roasted Monkfish. This recipe captures the essence of Etxebarri's commitment to simplicity, quality ingredients, and the primal art of open-fire cooking. Let the embers dance around the monkfish, creating a dish that is both elemental and extraordinary.

Serving: 4 servings
Preparation Time: 20 minutes
Ready Time: 45 minutes

Ingredients:
- 4 monkfish fillets (about 6 ounces each)
- 1/4 cup extra-virgin olive oil
- 2 teaspoons sea salt
- 1 teaspoon freshly ground black pepper
- 1 teaspoon smoked paprika
- 1 lemon, thinly sliced
- Fresh parsley for garnish

Instructions:
1. Preheat your grill or charcoal barbecue until the embers are glowing, creating a medium-high heat.
2. In a small bowl, combine the olive oil, sea salt, black pepper, and smoked paprika. Mix well to create a flavorful marinade.
3. Pat the monkfish fillets dry with paper towels. Brush the fillets with the prepared marinade, ensuring they are well-coated on both sides.
4. Place the monkfish fillets directly on the grill grates, allowing them to cook over the embers. Add lemon slices to the grill alongside the fillets.
5. Grill the monkfish for about 6-8 minutes per side or until the fish is opaque and easily flakes with a fork. The lemon slices should also be grilled until they develop grill marks.
6. Once cooked, remove the monkfish from the grill and transfer to a serving platter. Garnish with grilled lemon slices and fresh parsley.
7. Serve the Ember-Roasted Monkfish hot, allowing the smoky aroma to entice your senses.

Nutrition Information:
(Per Serving)

- Calories: 280 kcal
- Protein: 28g
- Fat: 17g
- Saturated Fat: 2.5g
- Carbohydrates: 3g
- Fiber: 1g
- Sugars: 1g
- Cholesterol: 70mg
- Sodium: 980mg

Elevate your dining experience with the Ember-Roasted Monkfish, a dish that encapsulates the soulful essence of Asador Etxebarri's culinary expertise.

28. Charcoal-Grilled Hake

Indulge your taste buds in the smoky essence of Spain with this exquisite recipe inspired by the renowned Asador Etxebarri in Axpe. Charcoal-Grilled Hake embodies the rustic charm and culinary prowess of this iconic establishment, offering a symphony of flavors that dance on your palate. Prepare to embark on a gastronomic journey that captures the essence of Basque cuisine, celebrating the simplicity of fresh ingredients and the mastery of charcoal grilling.

Serving: 4 servings
Preparation Time: 15 minutes
Ready Time: 45 minutes

Ingredients:
- 4 fresh hake fillets (about 6 ounces each)
- 2 tablespoons olive oil
- 1 teaspoon sea salt
- 1/2 teaspoon freshly ground black pepper
- 1 lemon, sliced for garnish
- Fresh parsley, chopped, for garnish

Instructions:
1. Prepare the Charcoal Grill:

- Start by lighting a charcoal grill and allowing the coals to burn until they are covered with white ash. This ensures a consistent and even heat for grilling.

2. Season the Hake:
- Brush each hake fillet with olive oil, ensuring they are evenly coated.
- Season the fillets with sea salt and freshly ground black pepper, covering both sides for a well-balanced flavor.

3. Grill the Hake:
- Place the hake fillets on the preheated charcoal grill, positioning them directly over the hot coals.
- Grill the fillets for approximately 4-5 minutes per side or until the fish is opaque and easily flakes with a fork. The grill's smoky aroma will infuse the hake with a distinctive flavor.

4. Garnish and Serve:
- Transfer the grilled hake fillets to a serving platter.
- Garnish with slices of lemon and a sprinkle of freshly chopped parsley to add a burst of freshness and visual appeal.

5. Serve Warm:
- Serve the Charcoal-Grilled Hake immediately while it's still warm. The contrast of the smoky char and the delicate flavor of the fish will captivate your taste buds.

Nutrition Information:
- *Per Serving:*
- Calories: 250
- Protein: 28g
- Carbohydrates: 1g
- Fat: 15g
- Saturated Fat: 2g
- Cholesterol: 70mg
- Sodium: 600mg
- Fiber: 0g
- Sugar: 0g

Elevate your culinary skills and savor the essence of Asador Etxebarri with this Charcoal-Grilled Hake recipe. A celebration of simplicity and bold flavors, this dish is sure to transport you to the heart of Basque culinary excellence.

29. Grilled Sea Bass with Herbs

Indulge in the rustic flavors of the Basque Country with this exquisite recipe inspired by the renowned Asador Etxebarri in Axpe, Spain. Grilled Sea Bass with Herbs is a celebration of simplicity and quality ingredients, reflecting the essence of the restaurant's menu. The smoky aroma and delicate infusion of herbs elevate this dish to a culinary masterpiece that captures the essence of Basque cuisine.

Serving: 4 servings
Preparation Time: 15 minutes
Ready Time: 30 minutes

Ingredients:
- 4 sea bass fillets (6 ounces each)
- 2 tablespoons olive oil
- 1 tablespoon fresh lemon juice
- Salt and black pepper to taste

Herb Marinade:
- 2 cloves garlic, minced
- 2 tablespoons fresh parsley, finely chopped
- 1 tablespoon fresh thyme leaves
- 1 tablespoon fresh rosemary, finely chopped
- Zest of 1 lemon
- 1/4 cup extra virgin olive oil

Instructions:
1. Prepare the Herb Marinade:
- In a small bowl, combine minced garlic, chopped parsley, thyme leaves, rosemary, lemon zest, and extra virgin olive oil. Mix well to create a fragrant herb marinade.
2. Marinate the Sea Bass:
- Place the sea bass fillets in a shallow dish.
- Brush each fillet with olive oil and lemon juice.
- Season with salt and black pepper.
- Generously coat the fillets with the herb marinade, ensuring an even distribution.
- Allow the sea bass to marinate for at least 15 minutes to absorb the flavors.
3. Preheat the Grill:

- Preheat your grill to medium-high heat. Ensure the grates are clean and lightly oiled to prevent sticking.

4. Grill the Sea Bass:
- Place the marinated sea bass fillets on the preheated grill.
- Grill for approximately 4-5 minutes per side or until the fish easily flakes with a fork.
- The herbs will create a tantalizing crust while the grill imparts a subtle smokiness.

5. Serve:
- Gently transfer the grilled sea bass to serving plates.
- Drizzle with any remaining herb marinade for an extra burst of flavor.

Nutrition Information:
- *Note: Nutritional values may vary based on specific ingredients used.*
- Calories: XXX per serving
- Protein: XXX g
- Fat: XXX g
- Carbohydrates: XXX g
- Fiber: XXX g
- Sugar: XXX g
- Sodium: XXX mg

Enjoy the Grilled Sea Bass with Herbs, a culinary journey inspired by the iconic Asador Etxebarri, bringing the tastes of Axpe, Spain, to your dining table.

30. Oak-Grilled Sole

Experience the rustic flavors of the Basque Country with our Oak-Grilled Sole recipe, inspired by the renowned Asador Etxebarri in Axpe, Spain. This dish captures the essence of traditional Spanish cuisine, where simplicity meets exceptional taste. The oak-grilled sole is a testament to the restaurant's commitment to using high-quality ingredients and mastering the art of open-fire cooking.

Serving: Serves 4
Preparation Time: 15 minutes
Ready Time: 30 minutes

Ingredients:
- 4 whole sole, cleaned and scaled
- 1/4 cup olive oil
- 2 cloves garlic, minced
- 1 tablespoon fresh parsley, chopped
- 1 lemon, sliced
- Salt and pepper to taste
- Oak wood chips for grilling

Instructions:
1. Prepare the Oak Wood Chips:
- Soak the oak wood chips in water for at least 30 minutes. This will ensure a slow, steady release of smoke during grilling.
2. Preheat the Grill:
- Prepare a charcoal or gas grill for direct grilling over medium-high heat. Add the soaked oak wood chips to the charcoal for a smoky flavor.
3. Prepare the Sole:
- Make diagonal cuts on both sides of each sole, allowing the flavors to penetrate. Season both sides with salt and pepper.
4. Garlic and Olive Oil Mixture:
- In a small bowl, mix the minced garlic with olive oil. Brush this mixture over the sole, ensuring it reaches the cuts for added flavor.
5. Grilling the Sole:
- Place the sole on the preheated grill grates. Grill for about 5-7 minutes per side or until the fish is cooked through and has a beautiful smoky char.
6. Garnish and Serve:
- Remove the oak-grilled sole from the grill and place on a serving platter. Sprinkle with fresh chopped parsley and garnish with lemon slices.

Nutrition Information:
- *(Per Serving)*
- Calories: XXX
- Protein: XXXg
- Fat: XXXg
- Carbohydrates: XXXg
- Fiber: XXXg
- Sugar: XXXg
- Sodium: XXXmg

Note: The nutrition information is an estimate and may vary based on specific ingredients used.

Indulge in the rich, smoky aroma and savory flavors of Oak-Grilled Sole—a dish that pays homage to the culinary mastery of Asador Etxebarri. Enjoy this delightful creation with friends and family, savoring every bite of its simplicity and authenticity.

31. Ember-Cooked Codfish

Embark on a culinary journey inspired by the rustic charm of Asador Etxebarri in Axpe, Spain. Known for their mastery in ember-cooking, this recipe brings you the essence of their renowned menu. The Ember-Cooked Codfish perfectly captures the smoky flavors and traditional techniques that define the Asador Etxebarri experience.

Serving: 4 servings
Preparation Time: 20 minutes
Ready Time: 40 minutes

Ingredients:
- 4 codfish fillets (6 oz each)
- 1/4 cup olive oil
- 2 cloves garlic, minced
- 1 teaspoon smoked paprika
- 1 teaspoon sea salt
- 1/2 teaspoon black pepper
- 1 lemon, thinly sliced
- Fresh parsley for garnish

Instructions:
1. Prepare the Ember Bed:
- If you have a charcoal grill, light the charcoal and let it burn until covered with white ash. If using a gas grill, set it to medium-high heat.
- Arrange the charcoal on one side of the grill, creating a hot and a cooler zone. This will allow for controlled ember cooking.
2. Season the Codfish:
- Pat the codfish fillets dry with paper towels.

- In a small bowl, mix olive oil, minced garlic, smoked paprika, sea salt, and black pepper.
- Brush the codfish fillets with the seasoned olive oil mixture, ensuring they are well coated.

3. Cooking Over Embers:
- Place the codfish fillets on the cooler zone of the grill, allowing them to cook indirectly over the embers.
- Close the lid and cook for about 15-20 minutes, or until the codfish is opaque and flakes easily with a fork.

4. Infuse with Smoky Aroma:
- During the last 5 minutes of cooking, carefully move the codfish fillets to the hot zone of the grill to give them a delightful smoky finish.
- Add lemon slices to the grill for a minute on each side, until they develop a light char.

5. Serve with Elegance:
- Gently transfer the ember-cooked codfish to serving plates.
- Garnish with grilled lemon slices and fresh parsley.

Nutrition Information:
- *Note: Nutritional values are approximate and may vary.*
- Calories per serving: 250
- Protein: 28g
- Fat: 12g
- Carbohydrates: 3g
- Fiber: 1g
- Sugar: 0g
- Sodium: 600mg

Elevate your dining experience with this Ember-Cooked Codfish recipe, reminiscent of the flavors that make Asador Etxebarri a culinary haven in Axpe, Spain. Enjoy the smoky richness and succulence that ember-cooking imparts to this delightful dish.

32. Grilled Red Mullet

Indulge your taste buds in the rich culinary heritage of Spain with this Grilled Red Mullet recipe inspired by the renowned menu of Restaurant Asador Etxebarri in Axpe. Known for their commitment to enhancing natural flavors through traditional grilling techniques, this dish captures the essence of Spanish gastronomy. The Grilled Red Mullet showcases the restaurant's dedication to using fresh, high-quality ingredients to create an exquisite and memorable dining experience.

Serving: 4 servings
Preparation Time: 15 minutes
Ready Time: 30 minutes

Ingredients:
- 4 whole Red Mullets, cleaned and gutted
- 2 tablespoons olive oil
- 2 cloves garlic, minced
- 1 teaspoon smoked paprika
- 1 teaspoon sea salt
- 1/2 teaspoon black pepper
- Fresh parsley, chopped (for garnish)
- Lemon wedges (for serving)

Instructions:
1. Preheat the grill to medium-high heat.
2. In a small bowl, combine olive oil, minced garlic, smoked paprika, sea salt, and black pepper to create a flavorful marinade.
3. Pat the red mullets dry with paper towels. Brush the marinade generously over each fish, ensuring it coats both sides.
4. Place the marinated red mullets on the preheated grill, allowing them to cook for approximately 5-7 minutes per side or until the flesh is opaque and easily flakes with a fork. The skin should be crispy and slightly charred.
5. Carefully remove the grilled red mullets from the grill and transfer them to a serving platter.
6. Garnish with freshly chopped parsley and serve with lemon wedges on the side for a zesty touch.

Nutrition Information:
(Per Serving)
- Calories: 220 kcal
- Protein: 26g
- Fat: 12g
- Saturated Fat: 2g
- Cholesterol: 60mg

- Carbohydrates: 1g
- Fiber: 0g
- Sugars: 0g
- Sodium: 650mg

Embrace the flavors of Asador Etxebarri in your own kitchen with this Grilled Red Mullet recipe—a tribute to the culinary excellence that defines Spanish dining.

33. Fire-Grilled Grouper

Inspired by the culinary excellence of Asador Etxebarri in Axpe, Spain, this Fire-Grilled Grouper recipe brings the essence of Basque Country dining to your own kitchen. Asador Etxebarri is renowned for its commitment to using top-quality ingredients and traditional grilling techniques, and this dish pays homage to their mastery of open-flame cooking. Enjoy the rich flavors and smoky aromas as you recreate this delectable Fire-Grilled Grouper in the comfort of your home.

Serving: 4 servings
Preparation Time: 15 minutes
Ready Time: 30 minutes

Ingredients:
- 4 grouper fillets (6-8 ounces each)
- 2 tablespoons olive oil
- 1 teaspoon smoked paprika
- 1 teaspoon sea salt
- 1/2 teaspoon black pepper
- 1 lemon, sliced for garnish
- Fresh parsley, chopped (for garnish)

Instructions:
1. Prepare the Grill:
Preheat your grill to medium-high heat, ensuring the grates are clean and well-oiled.
2. Season the Grouper:

In a small bowl, combine olive oil, smoked paprika, sea salt, and black pepper. Brush the mixture generously over both sides of the grouper fillets, ensuring they are evenly coated.

3. Grill the Grouper:

Place the seasoned grouper fillets on the preheated grill. Grill each side for about 4-5 minutes or until the fish is opaque and easily flakes with a fork. The grilling time may vary based on the thickness of the fillets.

4. Garnish and Serve:

Once the grouper is grilled to perfection, transfer it to a serving platter. Garnish with lemon slices and a sprinkle of fresh chopped parsley for a burst of freshness.

5. Serve Immediately:

Fire-Grilled Grouper is best enjoyed hot off the grill. Serve it immediately, and savor the smoky flavors that evoke the essence of Asador Etxebarri's culinary mastery.

Nutrition Information:

Note: Nutritional values are approximate and may vary based on specific ingredients used.

- Calories: 250 per serving
- Protein: 30g
- Fat: 12g
- Carbohydrates: 2g
- Fiber: 1g
- Sugars: 0g
- Cholesterol: 60mg
- Sodium: 600mg

Bring the rustic charm of Asador Etxebarri to your table with this Fire-Grilled Grouper recipe – a delightful dish that captures the essence of Basque Country's culinary traditions.

34. Ember-Roasted John Dory

Experience the rustic flavors of the Basque Country with this exquisite Ember-Roasted John Dory recipe, inspired by the renowned menu of Asador Etxebarri in Axpe, Spain. Asador Etxebarri is celebrated for its commitment to traditional grilling techniques, using open flames and carefully selected ingredients to create dishes that capture the essence of the region. In this recipe, the delicate and flaky John Dory fish is elevated to new heights through the mesmerizing touch of ember-roasting, resulting in a dish that pays homage to the culinary heritage of the Basque Country.

Serving: 4 servings
Preparation Time: 15 minutes
Ready Time: 45 minutes

Ingredients:
- 4 fresh John Dory fillets
- Sea salt, to taste
- Freshly ground black pepper, to taste
- 2 tablespoons olive oil
- 1 lemon, sliced for garnish

Instructions:
1. Preheat your grill or barbecue to medium-high heat, allowing the embers to develop.
2. Season the John Dory fillets with sea salt and freshly ground black pepper, ensuring an even coating on both sides.
3. Drizzle the fillets with olive oil, gently rubbing it into the flesh to enhance the flavors.
4. Place the seasoned fillets directly on the grill grates, over the open flames. Allow the embers to impart a smoky, charred essence to the fish.
5. Grill the fillets for approximately 4-5 minutes on each side or until the fish is opaque and easily flakes with a fork.
6. Remove the ember-roasted John Dory from the grill and transfer to a serving platter. Garnish with sliced lemons for a burst of citrus freshness.
7. Serve immediately, allowing the subtle smokiness of the ember-roasting to take center stage.

Nutrition Information:
(Per Serving)
- Calories: 220 kcal
- Protein: 28g
- Fat: 11g
- Carbohydrates: 2g
- Fiber: 1g
- Sugars: 0g

- Cholesterol: 60mg
- Sodium: 450mg

Elevate your dining experience with this Ember-Roasted John Dory, a testament to the culinary mastery of Asador Etxebarri and the rich gastronomic traditions of the Basque Country.

35. Oak-Grilled Salmon

Elevate your culinary experience with the exquisite flavors of Oak-Grilled Salmon, inspired by the renowned menu of Restaurant Asador Etxebarri in Axpe, Spain. This dish embodies the essence of traditional Basque cuisine, where the simplicity of fresh ingredients meets the artistry of oak grilling. Immerse yourself in the smoky, rich taste of perfectly grilled salmon that captures the essence of the rustic charm of Etxebarri's offerings.

Serving: Serves 4
Preparation Time: 15 minutes
Ready Time: 30 minutes

Ingredients:
- 4 salmon fillets (6 ounces each), skin-on
- 1 tablespoon olive oil
- Salt and black pepper, to taste
- 1 lemon, sliced for garnish

Instructions:
1. Prepare the Oak Grill: Preheat your oak grill to medium-high heat, ensuring the coals are evenly distributed for consistent cooking.
2. Prepare the Salmon: Rub each salmon fillet with olive oil, and season generously with salt and black pepper. Allow the salmon to sit at room temperature for 10 minutes to absorb the flavors.
3. Grill the Salmon: Place the salmon fillets on the preheated grill, skin side down. Grill for approximately 4-5 minutes per side, or until the salmon is cooked to your desired level of doneness. The oak grilling will impart a smoky flavor and a beautifully charred exterior.
4. Serve: Transfer the grilled salmon to a serving platter, garnish with lemon slices, and serve immediately. The salmon's natural flavors,

enhanced by the oak grilling, will be a delightful addition to your dining experience.

Nutrition Information:
(Per Serving)
- Calories: 300
- Protein: 34g
- Fat: 18g
- Carbohydrates: 2g
- Fiber: 1g
- Sugar: 0g
- Sodium: 70mg

Indulge in the essence of Asador Etxebarri with this Oak-Grilled Salmon recipe, where simplicity meets sophistication on your plate. Enjoy the harmony of flavors and the cultural richness of Axpe, Spain, right in the comfort of your home.

36. Grilled Wild Trout

Elevate your culinary experience with the inspired flavors of Asador Etxebarri, Axpe, Spain. Our Grilled Wild Trout recipe captures the essence of this renowned restaurant, known for its commitment to using high-quality, local ingredients and embracing the simplicity of wood-fired grilling. Immerse yourself in the rich traditions of Basque cuisine as you savor the delicate and smoky nuances of grilled wild trout.

Serving: Serves 4
Preparation Time: 15 minutes
Ready Time: 30 minutes

Ingredients:
- 4 whole wild trout, cleaned and scaled
- 2 tablespoons olive oil
- 2 teaspoons sea salt
- 1 teaspoon freshly ground black pepper
- 1 lemon, thinly sliced
- Fresh herbs (such as thyme or rosemary) for garnish

Instructions:

1. Prepare the Grill:
Preheat a charcoal or wood-fired grill to medium-high heat. The wood smoke will impart a unique flavor to the trout.

2. Prepare the Trout:
Rinse the trout under cold water and pat them dry with paper towels. Rub the exterior and cavity of each trout with olive oil, ensuring an even coating.

3. Season the Trout:
Sprinkle sea salt and freshly ground black pepper evenly over the trout, both inside and out. Be generous with the seasoning to enhance the natural flavors of the fish.

4. Stuff with Lemon:
Place a few slices of lemon inside the cavity of each trout. The citrusy notes will infuse the fish with brightness as it grills.

5. Grill the Trout:
Carefully place the seasoned trout on the preheated grill grates. Grill for approximately 5-7 minutes per side, or until the flesh is opaque and easily flakes with a fork. Adjust the cooking time based on the size of the trout.

6. Garnish and Serve:
Transfer the grilled trout to a serving platter, garnish with fresh herbs, and serve immediately. The crisp skin and smoky flavor will transport you to the heart of Basque country.

Nutrition Information:

Note: Nutrition information is approximate and may vary based on specific ingredients used.

- Calories per serving: 250
- Protein: 30g
- Fat: 14g
- Carbohydrates: 2g
- Fiber: 1g
- Sugars: 0g
- Cholesterol: 80mg
- Sodium: 600mg

Indulge in the rustic charm and exquisite taste of Grilled Wild Trout, a dish that pays homage to the culinary mastery of Asador Etxebarri in Axpe, Spain.

37. Wood-Grilled Eel

Indulge your senses in the rustic flavors of Spain with this exquisite Wood-Grilled Eel recipe, inspired by the culinary mastery of Restaurant Asador Etxebarri in Axpe. Known for its commitment to traditional techniques and high-quality ingredients, Asador Etxebarri's menu is a celebration of the elemental art of wood grilling. This dish captures the essence of their approach, delivering a smoky symphony of flavors that dance on the palate.

Serving: 4 servings
Preparation Time: 20 minutes
Ready Time: 2 hours (including marination time)

Ingredients:
- 4 fresh eels, cleaned and gutted
- 1/4 cup olive oil
- 2 tablespoons honey
- 2 tablespoons soy sauce
- 1 tablespoon smoked paprika
- 1 teaspoon black pepper, freshly ground
- 1 teaspoon sea salt
- 1 lemon, sliced (for garnish)
- Fresh parsley, chopped (for garnish)

Instructions:
1. Prepare the Eels:
- Ensure the eels are thoroughly cleaned and gutted. Pat them dry with paper towels.
2. Marinate the Eels:
- In a bowl, whisk together olive oil, honey, soy sauce, smoked paprika, black pepper, and sea salt to create a marinade.
- Place the eels in a shallow dish and generously coat them with the marinade. Let them marinate for at least 1 hour, allowing the flavors to infuse.
3. Preheat the Grill:
- Prepare a wood-fired grill, allowing the flames to subside and the coals to turn into glowing embers. The eels will be grilled directly over the wood for an authentic smoky flavor.
4. Grill the Eels:

- Place the marinated eels on the grill grates, cooking for about 8-10 minutes per side or until they are cooked through and have a delightful smoky char.

5. Garnish and Serve:
- Transfer the wood-grilled eels to a serving platter. Garnish with lemon slices and freshly chopped parsley for a burst of freshness.

6. Enjoy:
- Serve hot and savor the unique blend of smokiness and marinade that defines this Wood-Grilled Eel dish, reminiscent of the culinary excellence found at Asador Etxebarri.

Nutrition Information:
(Per Serving)
- Calories: 350
- Protein: 25g
- Fat: 20g
- Carbohydrates: 15g
- Fiber: 2g
- Sugar: 10g
- Sodium: 800mg

Elevate your home cooking with this Wood-Grilled Eel recipe, a homage to the gastronomic wonders of Asador Etxebarri. Each bite is a journey to the heart of Spanish culinary tradition, where simplicity and fire combine to create unforgettable flavors.

38. Ember-Grilled Anchovies

Embark on a culinary journey inspired by the exquisite menu of Asador Etxebarri in Axpe, Spain, where tradition and innovation converge over open flames. One dish that captures the essence of this exceptional dining experience is the Ember-Grilled Anchovies. This recipe pays homage to the mastery of open-fire cooking, infusing the delicate flavor of anchovies with the smoky allure of ember-grilling.

Serving: 4 servings
Preparation Time: 15 minutes
Ready Time: 25 minutes

Ingredients:
- 16 fresh anchovies, cleaned and gutted
- 2 tablespoons extra-virgin olive oil
- 1 teaspoon sea salt
- 1/2 teaspoon freshly ground black pepper
- 1 lemon, cut into wedges for serving

Instructions:
1. Prepare the Ember Grill: If you have an ember grill or charcoal grill, light it and let the embers burn down until they are covered with a layer of white ash. The heat should be medium-high.
2. Season the Anchovies: Rinse the anchovies under cold water and pat them dry with paper towels. In a bowl, toss the anchovies with olive oil, sea salt, and black pepper, ensuring they are evenly coated.
3. Grill the Anchovies: Place the seasoned anchovies directly on the grill grates, laying them perpendicular to the bars to prevent sticking. Grill for 2-3 minutes per side until the flesh is opaque and easily flakes with a fork. The skin should be slightly charred, imparting a smoky flavor to the fish.
4. Serve: Arrange the ember-grilled anchovies on a platter and garnish with lemon wedges. Drizzle with a bit of extra-virgin olive oil for an added touch of richness.
5. Enjoy: Dive into the unique combination of smokiness and brininess as you savor each ember-grilled anchovy. Serve as a tapa, appetizer, or part of a Mediterranean-inspired feast.

Nutrition Information:
(Per serving)
- Calories: 180
- Total Fat: 12g
- Saturated Fat: 2g
- Trans Fat: 0g
- Cholesterol: 45mg
- Sodium: 620mg
- Total Carbohydrates: 1g
- Dietary Fiber: 0g
- Sugars: 0g
- Protein: 18g

Note: Nutrition information is approximate and may vary based on specific ingredients used.

39. Grilled Mussels with Seaweed

Elevate your culinary experience with this exquisite recipe inspired by the renowned menu of Asador Etxebarri in Axpe, Spain. The Grilled Mussels with Seaweed brings together the freshness of the sea and the rustic charm of Spanish cuisine. This dish pays homage to the culinary mastery of Asador Etxebarri, where every ingredient is treated with the utmost respect, resulting in a symphony of flavors that dance on your palate.

Serving: 4 servings
Preparation Time: 20 minutes
Ready Time: 30 minutes

Ingredients:
- 2 pounds fresh mussels, cleaned and debearded
- 1/4 cup extra virgin olive oil
- 2 tablespoons finely chopped fresh seaweed (such as dulse or nori)
- 2 cloves garlic, minced
- 1/4 cup finely chopped fresh parsley
- 1/2 teaspoon smoked paprika
- Salt and black pepper to taste
- Lemon wedges for serving

Instructions:
1. Prepare the Grill:
Preheat your grill to medium-high heat.
2. Clean and Debeard the Mussels:
Rinse the fresh mussels under cold running water, scrubbing off any debris. Remove the beards by pulling them away from the shell. Discard any mussels with open or cracked shells.
3. Prepare the Marinade:
In a small bowl, combine the olive oil, chopped seaweed, minced garlic, chopped parsley, smoked paprika, salt, and black pepper. Mix well to create a flavorful marinade.
4. Coat the Mussels:

Place the cleaned mussels in a large bowl. Pour the marinade over the mussels, ensuring they are well-coated. Allow them to marinate for about 10 minutes, letting the flavors meld.

5. Grill the Mussels:

Arrange the mussels on the preheated grill grates. Grill for 2-3 minutes per side or until the shells open and the mussels are cooked through. Discard any unopened shells.

6. Serve:

Transfer the grilled mussels to a serving platter. Drizzle any remaining marinade over the top. Serve hot with lemon wedges on the side.

Nutrition Information:
(Per Serving)
- Calories: 280
- Protein: 20g
- Carbohydrates: 8g
- Fat: 18g
- Saturated Fat: 3g
- Cholesterol: 50mg
- Sodium: 600mg
- Fiber: 2g
- Sugar: 1g

Savor the essence of Asador Etxebarri in every bite of these Grilled Mussels with Seaweed—a dish that captures the soul of Spanish cuisine.

40. Smoked Herring

Inspired by the culinary delights of Asador Etxebarri in Axpe, Spain, this Smoked Herring recipe pays homage to the restaurant's commitment to quality and traditional Basque cooking techniques. The rich, smoky flavors of the herring, combined with a touch of Spanish flair, make this dish a true celebration of regional gastronomy.

Serving: 4 servings
Preparation Time: 15 minutes
Ready Time: 2 hours (including smoking time)

Ingredients:

- 4 whole fresh herring, gutted and scaled
- 1 cup coarse sea salt
- 1 cup brown sugar
- 1 tablespoon black pepper, coarsely ground
- 1 tablespoon paprika
- 1 teaspoon garlic powder
- 1 teaspoon onion powder
- Olive oil, for brushing
- Wood chips for smoking (preferably oak or fruitwood)

Instructions:

1. Prepare the Herring:
- Rinse the herring under cold water and pat them dry with paper towels.
- Make deep diagonal cuts on both sides of each fish, ensuring the cuts penetrate to the bone.

2. Brine the Herring:
- In a bowl, combine sea salt, brown sugar, black pepper, paprika, garlic powder, and onion powder.
- Rub the herring generously with the spice mixture, making sure to get the seasoning into the cuts.
- Place the herring in a shallow dish, cover, and refrigerate for at least 1 hour to allow the flavors to meld.

3. Prepare the Smoker:
- Soak wood chips in water for at least 30 minutes.
- Set up your smoker according to the manufacturer's instructions. Preheat to 200°F (93°C).

4. Smoke the Herring:
- Brush the herring with olive oil to prevent sticking.
- Place the herring on the smoker grates and add the soaked wood chips.
- Smoke the herring for approximately 1 to 1.5 hours, or until they reach an internal temperature of 145°F (63°C).

5. Finish and Serve:
- Once smoked, carefully remove the herring from the smoker.
- Allow them to rest for a few minutes before serving.
- Drizzle with a bit of olive oil before serving for added richness.

Nutrition Information:

(Per serving)
- Calories: 280
- Protein: 20g

- Fat: 18g
- Carbohydrates: 8g
- Fiber: 1g
- Sugar: 6g
- Sodium: 3200mg

This Smoked Herring dish captures the essence of Asador Etxebarri, delivering a culinary experience that showcases the simplicity and brilliance of Basque cuisine. Serve it with crusty bread and a side salad for a complete and satisfying meal.

41. Charcoal-Grilled Oily Fish Salad

Indulge in the rustic flavors of the Basque Country with this Charcoal-Grilled Oily Fish Salad, inspired by the renowned Asador Etxebarri in Axpe, Spain. A homage to their mastery of open-flame cooking, this dish captures the essence of smoky, chargrilled goodness combined with the freshness of a vibrant salad. The star of the show is the perfectly grilled oily fish, which takes center stage amidst a medley of crisp vegetables and zesty dressing. Elevate your dining experience with this simple yet sophisticated recipe that brings the essence of Asador Etxebarri to your own kitchen.

Serving: 4 servings
Preparation Time: 20 minutes
Ready Time: 30 minutes

Ingredients:
- 4 oily fish fillets (such as mackerel or sardines)
- 2 tablespoons olive oil
- Salt and black pepper to taste
- 1 teaspoon smoked paprika
- 1 lemon, sliced for garnish

For the Salad:
- Mixed salad greens (arugula, watercress, and spinach work well)
- 1 cucumber, thinly sliced
- 1 red onion, thinly sliced
- 1 cup cherry tomatoes, halved
- 1/4 cup Kalamata olives, pitted

- 1/4 cup fresh parsley, chopped

For the Dressing:
- 3 tablespoons extra virgin olive oil
- 2 tablespoons red wine vinegar
- 1 teaspoon Dijon mustard
- 1 clove garlic, minced
- Salt and pepper to taste

Instructions:
1. Preheat your charcoal grill to medium-high heat.
2. Pat the fish fillets dry with a paper towel and rub them with olive oil. Season with salt, pepper, and smoked paprika.
3. Place the fish fillets on the preheated grill and cook for 3-4 minutes per side or until they are cooked through and have a beautiful char.
4. In a large bowl, combine the mixed salad greens, cucumber, red onion, cherry tomatoes, olives, and fresh parsley.
5. In a small bowl, whisk together the extra virgin olive oil, red wine vinegar, Dijon mustard, minced garlic, salt, and pepper to create the dressing.
6. Drizzle the dressing over the salad and toss gently to combine.
7. Once the fish is ready, place it on top of the salad. Garnish with lemon slices.
8. Serve the Charcoal-Grilled Oily Fish Salad immediately, allowing the smoky flavors to mingle with the crisp salad.

Nutrition Information:
(Per serving)
- Calories: 300
- Protein: 20g
- Fat: 22g
- Carbohydrates: 10g
- Fiber: 3g
- Sugar: 4g
- Sodium: 450mg

Elevate your dining experience with this Charcoal-Grilled Oily Fish Salad, a tribute to the culinary excellence of Asador Etxebarri, and savor the symphony of flavors inspired by the Basque tradition of open-flame cooking.

42. Grilled Iberian Ham

Elevate your culinary experience with the smoky and savory delight of Grilled Iberian Ham, a masterpiece inspired by the renowned menu of Restaurant Asador Etxebarri in Axpe, Spain. Asador Etxebarri is celebrated for its commitment to grilling perfection, and this dish pays homage to the rich flavors and culinary traditions of the region. The unparalleled quality of Iberian ham, expertly grilled to perfection, makes this dish a true delicacy for any occasion.

Serving: 4 servings
Preparation Time: 15 minutes
Ready Time: 30 minutes

Ingredients:
- 8 slices of high-quality Iberian ham
- 1 tablespoon olive oil
- Freshly ground black pepper, to taste

Instructions:
1. Prepare the Grill: Preheat your grill to medium-high heat. If using a charcoal grill, ensure the coals are evenly distributed for an even cooking surface.
2. Brush with Olive Oil: Lightly brush each slice of Iberian ham with olive oil on both sides. This will enhance the grilling process and add a subtle richness to the ham.
3. Grill the Iberian Ham: Place the ham slices on the preheated grill. Grill for approximately 1-2 minutes per side, or until the edges become slightly crispy and the ham develops a beautiful golden color.
4. Add Black Pepper: Sprinkle freshly ground black pepper over the grilled ham slices, adjusting to your desired level of spiciness.
5. Serve: Arrange the grilled Iberian ham on a platter and serve immediately. This dish is best enjoyed hot off the grill to savor the smoky essence and delicate flavors.

Nutrition Information:
Note: Nutritional values are approximate and may vary based on specific ingredients used.
- Calories per serving: 120
- Protein: 12g

- Fat: 7g
- Carbohydrates: 1g
- Fiber: 0g
- Sugar: 0g
- Sodium: 800mg

Indulge in the exquisite taste of Grilled Iberian Ham, a testament to the mastery of fire-infused culinary artistry showcased at Asador Etxebarri. This dish captures the essence of Spain's gastronomic heritage, inviting you to savor the simplicity and perfection of grilled perfection.

43. Oak-Smoked Chorizo

Transport your taste buds to the rustic charm of Spain with this exquisite Oak-Smoked Chorizo recipe, inspired by the renowned menu of Restaurant Asador Etxebarri in Axpe. This culinary masterpiece captures the essence of traditional Spanish flavors, combining the richness of chorizo with the subtle smokiness imparted by oak. Whether you're hosting a gathering or seeking to elevate your everyday meals, this Oak-Smoked Chorizo will undoubtedly become a showstopper at your table.

Serving: Ideal for sharing as a flavorful tapas dish, serve the Oak-Smoked Chorizo alongside crusty bread, olives, and a glass of your favorite Spanish red wine.
Preparation Time: 15 minutes (plus additional time for marination)
Ready Time: 24-48 hours (including marination and smoking time)

Ingredients:
- 1 pound (450g) Spanish-style cured chorizo
- 1 cup oak wood chips, soaked in water for 30 minutes
- 1 tablespoon sweet smoked paprika
- 1 teaspoon garlic powder
- 1 teaspoon dried oregano
- 1/2 teaspoon cayenne pepper (adjust to taste)
- 2 tablespoons olive oil

Instructions:

1. Prepare the Chorizo: Score the chorizo diagonally, creating shallow cuts to allow the flavors to penetrate. This step helps the chorizo absorb the smoky essence.
2. Create the Marinade: In a bowl, combine the sweet smoked paprika, garlic powder, dried oregano, cayenne pepper, and olive oil. Mix well to form a thick paste.
3. Coat the Chorizo: Massage the chorizo with the marinade, ensuring each piece is evenly coated. Place the chorizo in a shallow dish, cover, and refrigerate for at least 24 hours to allow the flavors to meld.
4. Prepare the Smoker: Preheat your smoker or grill to a low temperature. Add the soaked oak wood chips to the smoker box or directly onto the charcoal.
5. Smoke the Chorizo: Arrange the marinated chorizo on the smoker grates, maintaining a low heat. Close the lid and smoke for 2-3 hours, or until the chorizo develops a beautiful smoky crust.
6. Rest and Slice: Allow the Oak-Smoked Chorizo to rest for a few minutes before slicing it into thin rounds. The exterior should boast a deep, smoky color, while the inside remains succulent and flavorful.
7. Serve: Arrange the smoked chorizo on a platter and garnish with fresh herbs. Pair it with crusty bread, olives, and a drizzle of extra virgin olive oil.

Nutrition Information:
(Per Serving - based on 4 servings)
- Calories: 320
- Protein: 15g
- Fat: 26g
- Carbohydrates: 3g
- Fiber: 1g
- Sugars: 1g
- Sodium: 950mg

Elevate your culinary experience with this Oak-Smoked Chorizo, a testament to the flavors and traditions celebrated at Asador Etxebarri in Axpe, Spain.

44. Ember-Roasted Blood Sausage

Embark on a culinary journey to the heart of Axpe, Spain, with this Ember-Roasted Blood Sausage recipe inspired by the renowned menu of Restaurant Asador Etxebarri. Asador Etxebarri is celebrated for its mastery of live-fire cooking, infusing traditional Basque flavors into every dish. The Ember-Roasted Blood Sausage captures the essence of this rustic gastronomy, bringing smoky undertones and rich, savory notes to your table.

Serving: 4 servings
Preparation Time: 15 minutes
Ready Time: 45 minutes

Ingredients:
- 4 blood sausages
- 2 tablespoons olive oil
- 1 teaspoon smoked paprika
- Salt, to taste
- Freshly ground black pepper, to taste

Instructions:
1. Prepare the Grill:
- Preheat your grill to medium-high heat, allowing the embers to develop.
2. Score the Sausages:
- Using a sharp knife, make shallow diagonal cuts on the surface of each blood sausage. This helps the sausages cook evenly and allows the flavors to infuse.
3. Season the Sausages:
- Drizzle olive oil over the sausages, ensuring they are well-coated. Sprinkle smoked paprika, salt, and freshly ground black pepper to taste. Gently rub the seasonings into the cuts.
4. Ember-Roasting:
- Place the sausages directly on the grill grates, positioning them over the embers. Allow them to cook for approximately 15-20 minutes, turning occasionally to achieve a crispy, golden exterior.
5. Monitor Cooking:
- Keep a close eye on the sausages to prevent burning. The goal is to achieve a crisp outer layer while ensuring the interior is thoroughly cooked.
6. Check Doneness:

- Confirm the sausages are cooked through by inserting a meat thermometer; it should register at least 160°F (71°C).
7. Rest Before Serving:
- Remove the Ember-Roasted Blood Sausages from the grill and let them rest for a few minutes. This allows the juices to redistribute, enhancing flavor and tenderness.
8. Serve and Enjoy:
- Slice the sausages diagonally and arrange them on a serving platter. Garnish with fresh herbs if desired. Serve immediately, savoring the smoky goodness of this Asador Etxebarri-inspired dish.

Nutrition Information:
- *(Note: Nutritional values are approximate and may vary based on specific ingredients and cooking methods.)*
- Calories: 300 per serving
- Protein: 15g
- Fat: 25g
- Carbohydrates: 2g
- Fiber: 1g

Bring the flavors of Asador Etxebarri into your home with this Ember-Roasted Blood Sausage recipe, a testament to the artistry of live-fire cooking and the culinary heritage of Axpe, Spain.

45. Grilled Morcilla

Grilled Morcilla is a tantalizing dish that captures the essence of traditional Spanish cuisine. Inspired by the rustic charm of Asador Etxebarri, this recipe celebrates the rich flavors of morcilla, a Spanish blood sausage, grilled to perfection, offering a delightful blend of smokiness and savory notes.

Serving: 4 servings
Preparation time: 10 minutes
Ready time: 20 minutes

Ingredients:
- 4 links of Morcilla (Spanish blood sausage)
- Olive oil, for brushing

Instructions:
1. Prepare the Grill: Preheat your grill to medium-high heat, ensuring it's clean and well-oiled to prevent sticking.
2. Prep the Morcilla: Place the morcilla links on a plate. Prick the sausages with a fork in a few places to prevent bursting while grilling.
3. Grill the Morcilla: Lightly brush each morcilla link with olive oil. Place them on the preheated grill, allowing them to cook for about 8-10 minutes, turning occasionally. The sausages should be evenly cooked and slightly charred on the outside.
4. Check for Doneness: To ensure they're thoroughly cooked, use a meat thermometer. The internal temperature should reach 160°F (71°C).
5. Serve: Once done, remove the grilled morcilla from the heat and let them rest for a couple of minutes before serving.
6. Presentation: Serve the grilled morcilla hot, either on its own as a flavorful appetizer or as part of a larger Spanish-inspired meal.

Nutrition Information: *(approximate values per serving)*
- Calories: 250 kcal
- Protein: 12g
- Fat: 20g
- Carbohydrates: 5g
- Fiber: 1g
- Sugar: 0g
- Sodium: 600mg

This dish pairs exceptionally well with a side of crusty bread, grilled vegetables, or a fresh salad, offering a delightful taste of Spanish culinary heritage. Enjoy the smoky, savory goodness of this grilled morcilla as a tribute to the flavors of Asador Etxebarri!

46. Fire-Grilled Txistorra

The essence of Basque cuisine is captured in the fiery flavors of the Fire-Grilled Txistorra, a dish inspired by the renowned culinary heritage of Restaurant Asador Etxebarri in Axpe, Spain. This recipe pays homage to the rustic charm and bold tastes of this iconic eatery, where tradition meets innovation in a celebration of local ingredients and grilling mastery.

Serving: 4 servings
Preparation time: 15 minutes
Ready time: 25 minutes

Ingredients:
- 12-16 Txistorra sausages (Basque fresh chorizo)
- Olive oil, for brushing
- Sea salt, to taste

Instructions:
1. Prepare the Grill: Preheat your grill to medium-high heat, aiming for a temperature around 400°F (200°C).
2. Prepare the Txistorra: Prick the Txistorra sausages in a few places using a fork. This helps release excess fat while grilling.
3. Grill the Txistorra: Place the sausages on the preheated grill. Cook, turning occasionally, until they're evenly charred and cooked through, approximately 10-12 minutes.
4. Brush with Olive Oil: During the grilling process, brush the sausages lightly with olive oil. This helps enhance the flavors and ensures they don't dry out.
5. Season and Serve: Once the Txistorra sausages are cooked through and have achieved a delicious char, remove them from the grill. Sprinkle with a pinch of sea salt for an added burst of flavor.
6. Presentation: Arrange the grilled Txistorra sausages on a platter or individual plates, ready to serve.

Nutrition Information: *Please note, nutritional values may vary based on specific ingredients used and serving sizes.*
- Calories: Approximately 250 calories per serving
- Fat: Around 20g per serving
- Protein: About 10g per serving
- Carbohydrates: Roughly 2g per serving

Enjoy the smoky aroma and robust flavors of this Fire-Grilled Txistorra, a simple yet exquisite dish that embodies the culinary artistry of the Basque region.
Would you like any further details or adjustments to this recipe?

47. Wood-Grilled Lamb Chops

Delve into the rustic charm of Spanish cuisine with this recipe for Wood-Grilled Lamb Chops inspired by the renowned flavors of Asador Etxebarri in Axpe, Spain. Embracing the simplicity of quality ingredients and the art of wood-fire grilling, this dish encapsulates the essence of Basque culinary traditions.

Serving: This recipe serves 4 people.
Preparation Time: Preparation time: 15 minutes
Ready Time: Ready in 30 minutes

Ingredients:
- 8 lamb loin chops, about 1 1/2 inches thick
- 4 cloves garlic, minced
- 2 tablespoons fresh rosemary, chopped
- 1 tablespoon fresh thyme leaves
- 1/4 cup olive oil
- Salt and freshly ground black pepper to taste

Instructions:
1. Begin by preparing the marinade. In a bowl, combine the minced garlic, chopped rosemary, thyme leaves, olive oil, salt, and black pepper. Mix well to create a fragrant marinade.
2. Pat dry the lamb chops using paper towels. This helps the marinade adhere better to the meat.
3. Place the lamb chops in a shallow dish or a resealable plastic bag. Pour the marinade over the chops, ensuring they are evenly coated. Cover the dish or seal the bag and let the lamb marinate in the refrigerator for at least 2 hours, allowing the flavors to infuse.
4. Preheat your wood-fired grill to medium-high heat, aiming for a temperature of around 375-400°F (190-200°C). Ensure the grill grates are clean and well-oiled to prevent sticking.
5. Once the grill is ready, remove the lamb chops from the marinade and shake off any excess. Allow them to sit at room temperature for about 15 minutes before grilling.
6. Place the lamb chops on the grill and cook for about 4-5 minutes on each side for medium-rare doneness, adjusting the time for your desired level of doneness.

7. When ready, remove the lamb chops from the grill and let them rest for a few minutes before serving. This allows the juices to redistribute, ensuring a tender and flavorful bite.

8. Serve the wood-grilled lamb chops hot, garnished with a sprinkle of fresh herbs if desired. Accompany them with your choice of sides like roasted vegetables or a crisp salad to complement the rich flavors.

Nutrition Information:
Note: Nutritional values can vary based on the specific cuts of meat and ingredients used.

Per serving:
Calories: Approximately 350
Protein: Approximately 25g
Fat: Approximately 28g
Carbohydrates: Approximately 1g
Fiber: Approximately 0.5g

Enjoy the smoky aroma and robust taste of these wood-grilled lamb chops, a homage to the timeless culinary traditions of Asador Etxebarri!

48. Ember-Cooked Pork Ribs

Indulge your taste buds in the smoky essence of Spanish culinary mastery with our Ember-Cooked Pork Ribs, a dish inspired by the renowned Asador Etxebarri in Axpe, Spain. Asador Etxebarri has earned international acclaim for its commitment to simple, high-quality ingredients and traditional cooking techniques. This recipe pays homage to their expertise in coaxing bold flavors from the elemental power of fire. Prepare to embark on a culinary journey that captures the essence of the Basque country with every savory bite.

Serving: 4
Preparation Time: 15 minutes
Ready Time: 3 hours

Ingredients:
- 2 racks of pork ribs
- 1 tablespoon smoked paprika
- 1 tablespoon sweet paprika

- 1 tablespoon coarse sea salt
- 1 tablespoon black pepper, freshly ground
- 2 teaspoons garlic powder
- 1 teaspoon onion powder
- 1 teaspoon cayenne pepper (adjust to taste)
- 1/4 cup olive oil
- Wood ember chunks (oak or hickory) for cooking

Instructions:
1. Prepare the Ribs:
- Trim excess fat from the pork ribs, leaving a thin layer for flavor.
- Remove the membrane from the back of the ribs for a more tender result.
2. Create the Spice Rub:
- In a small bowl, combine smoked paprika, sweet paprika, sea salt, black pepper, garlic powder, onion powder, and cayenne pepper.
- Rub the spice mixture evenly over both sides of the ribs, ensuring full coverage.
3. Marinate the Ribs:
- Drizzle olive oil over the ribs, massaging it into the meat.
- Allow the ribs to marinate for at least 1 hour to let the flavors meld.
4. Prepare the Ember Bed:
- Ignite wood embers, allowing them to burn down to a glowing, even heat.
5. Cook the Ribs:
- Place the marinated ribs directly on the ember bed, ensuring they are evenly distributed.
- Cook the ribs for approximately 2 to 2.5 hours, turning occasionally, until the meat is tender and has a rich, smoky flavor.
6. Rest and Serve:
- Allow the ribs to rest for a few minutes before slicing them into individual portions.
- Serve hot, allowing the smoky aroma to tantalize your senses.

Nutrition Information (per serving):
- Calories: 450
- Protein: 25g
- Fat: 35g
- Carbohydrates: 5g
- Fiber: 1g

- Sugars: 0g

Immerse yourself in the rustic charm of ember-cooked pork ribs, a culinary masterpiece inspired by the timeless traditions of Asador Etxebarri.

49. Grilled Duck Breast

Indulge in the rich and smoky flavors of the Spanish countryside with this exquisite Grilled Duck Breast recipe, inspired by the culinary mastery of Restaurant Asador Etxebarri in Axpe, Spain. Renowned for their commitment to quality ingredients and traditional grilling techniques, this dish captures the essence of the restaurant's menu, transporting you to the heart of Basque Country with every succulent bite.

Serving: Serves 4
Preparation Time: 15 minutes
Ready Time: 45 minutes

Ingredients:
- 4 duck breasts, skin-on
- 2 tablespoons olive oil
- 1 teaspoon sea salt
- 1/2 teaspoon black pepper, freshly ground
- 2 teaspoons smoked paprika
- 1 teaspoon thyme, fresh and chopped
- 1 lemon, sliced for garnish

Instructions:
1. Begin by scoring the skin of each duck breast in a crosshatch pattern, being careful not to cut into the meat.
2. In a small bowl, combine olive oil, sea salt, black pepper, smoked paprika, and chopped thyme to create a marinade.
3. Rub the marinade generously over both sides of the duck breasts, ensuring each piece is well-coated. Allow the duck to marinate at room temperature for 15 minutes to absorb the flavors.
4. Preheat the grill to medium-high heat. If using a charcoal grill, wait until the coals are covered with white ash.

5. Place the duck breasts on the grill, skin-side down, and cook for approximately 8-10 minutes or until the skin is golden and crisp.
6. Flip the duck breasts and continue grilling for an additional 6-8 minutes for medium-rare doneness. Adjust the cooking time based on your preference.
7. Remove the duck from the grill and let it rest for 5 minutes before slicing.
8. Serve the Grilled Duck Breast slices on a platter, garnished with fresh lemon slices for a burst of citrusy brightness.

Nutrition Information:
Note: Nutrition information is approximate and may vary based on specific ingredients used.
- Calories per serving: 350
- Protein: 25g
- Fat: 27g
- Carbohydrates: 1g
- Fiber: 0.5g
- Sugar: 0g
- Sodium: 650mg

Elevate your culinary experience with this Grilled Duck Breast recipe, celebrating the time-honored grilling traditions of Asador Etxebarri. Enjoy the tantalizing blend of smoky, seasoned perfection that pays homage to the rustic charm of Axpe, Spain.

50. Oak-Grilled Quail

Embark on a culinary journey inspired by the renowned restaurant Asador Etxebarri in Axpe, Spain. This recipe brings the rustic charm of oak-grilled quail to your kitchen, capturing the essence of the restaurant's commitment to simple, quality ingredients and expertly crafted flavors. Elevate your dining experience with this delectable Oak-Grilled Quail that pays homage to the culinary excellence of Asador Etxebarri.

Serving: 4 servings
Preparation Time: 20 minutes
Ready Time: 1 hour and 10 minutes

Ingredients:
- 4 whole quails, cleaned and dressed
- 1/4 cup olive oil
- 2 cloves garlic, minced
- 1 teaspoon smoked paprika
- 1 teaspoon sea salt
- 1/2 teaspoon freshly ground black pepper
- 1 tablespoon fresh parsley, chopped (for garnish)

Instructions:
1. Prepare the Quail:
- Rinse the quails under cold water and pat them dry with paper towels.
- Using kitchen shears, remove the backbone from each quail and flatten them slightly by pressing down on the breastbone.
2. Marinate the Quail:
- In a small bowl, whisk together the olive oil, minced garlic, smoked paprika, sea salt, and black pepper.
- Rub the quails with the marinade, ensuring they are well-coated. Allow them to marinate for at least 30 minutes to let the flavors meld.
3. Preheat the Grill:
- Preheat an oak-fired grill to medium-high heat. The distinct smokiness from the oak will impart a unique flavor to the quail.
4. Grill the Quail:
- Place the marinated quails on the preheated grill, breast side down. Grill for 5-7 minutes on each side or until the internal temperature reaches 165°F (74°C).
5. Serve:
- Transfer the oak-grilled quail to a serving platter, garnish with chopped parsley, and serve hot. This dish pairs exceptionally well with a side of grilled vegetables or a light salad.

Nutrition Information:
(Per Serving)
- Calories: 350
- Protein: 30g
- Fat: 24g
- Carbohydrates: 1g
- Fiber: 0.5g
- Sugar: 0g
- Cholesterol: 110mg

- Sodium: 600mg

Indulge in the rich, smoky flavors of Asador Etxebarri's oak-grilled quail, bringing a taste of Spain to your own table. This dish is a celebration of simplicity and quality, ensuring a memorable dining experience for you and your guests.

51. Ember-Roasted Pigeon

Delight your senses with the rustic flavors of the Basque Country with this Ember-Roasted Pigeon recipe, inspired by the culinary artistry of Asador Etxebarri in Axpe, Spain. Asador Etxebarri, known for its dedication to live-fire cooking, brings a unique smokiness to each dish, and this Ember-Roasted Pigeon is no exception. The method of cooking over smoldering embers imparts a distinct flavor that elevates the rich taste of pigeon to new heights.

Serving: 4 servings
Preparation Time: 20 minutes
Ready Time: 1 hour 30 minutes

Ingredients:
- 4 whole pigeons, cleaned
- Salt and black pepper, to taste
- 1/4 cup olive oil
- 2 teaspoons smoked paprika
- 1 teaspoon ground cumin
- 1 teaspoon garlic powder
- 1 teaspoon onion powder
- 1/2 teaspoon cayenne pepper
- Fresh thyme sprigs for garnish

Instructions:
1. Prepare the Pigeons:
- Preheat the grill or barbecue to medium-high heat. Allow the embers to form, ensuring a consistent heat source.
- Season the pigeons generously with salt and black pepper, both inside and out.
2. Create the Spice Rub:

- In a small bowl, combine olive oil, smoked paprika, ground cumin, garlic powder, onion powder, and cayenne pepper. Mix well to form a paste.

3. Rub the Spice Mixture:
- Rub the spice mixture evenly over the pigeons, ensuring they are well-coated with the flavorful blend.

4. Ember-Roasting:
- Place the seasoned pigeons directly onto the embers of the grill or barbecue. Cook for about 15-20 minutes, turning occasionally, until the skin is golden brown and the meat is cooked through.

5. Rest and Garnish:
- Remove the pigeons from the heat and let them rest for 10 minutes before carving. Garnish with fresh thyme sprigs for a fragrant touch.

6. Serve:
- Serve the Ember-Roasted Pigeon hot, allowing the smoky aroma to entice your taste buds. Pair it with your favorite roasted vegetables or a light salad for a complete Basque-inspired meal.

Nutrition Information:
(Per Serving)
- Calories: 350
- Protein: 25g
- Fat: 22g
- Carbohydrates: 5g
- Fiber: 1g
- Sodium: 450mg

Enjoy the rich and smoky essence of Asador Etxebarri in the comfort of your own home with this Ember-Roasted Pigeon recipe. It's a culinary journey that captures the essence of traditional Basque cuisine.

52. Grilled Rabbit with Garlic

Discover the rustic flavors of the Basque Country with this exquisite recipe inspired by the renowned Asador Etxebarri in Axpe, Spain. Grilled Rabbit with Garlic captures the essence of traditional Spanish cuisine, blending the earthy richness of rabbit with the aromatic allure of garlic. Asador Etxebarri is celebrated for its commitment to showcasing the finest ingredients through expert grilling techniques, and this dish is no exception. Elevate your culinary experience with this tantalizing blend of smoky, grilled goodness.

Serving: 4 servings
Preparation Time: 20 minutes
Ready Time: 1 hour 30 minutes

Ingredients:
- 1 whole rabbit, cut into serving pieces
- 8 cloves garlic, minced
- 1/4 cup olive oil
- 2 tablespoons fresh rosemary, finely chopped
- Salt and black pepper, to taste
- 1 lemon, sliced for garnish

Instructions:
1. Preheat the Grill: Prepare a charcoal or gas grill for medium-high heat.
2. Marinate the Rabbit: In a bowl, combine minced garlic, olive oil, chopped rosemary, salt, and black pepper. Rub this mixture evenly over the rabbit pieces, ensuring they are well-coated. Allow the rabbit to marinate for at least 30 minutes to let the flavors meld.
3. Grill the Rabbit: Place the marinated rabbit pieces on the preheated grill. Grill for about 15-20 minutes, turning occasionally, until the rabbit is cooked through and has a beautiful golden-brown color. Ensure that the internal temperature reaches at least 160°F (71°C).
4. Garnish and Serve: Once grilled to perfection, transfer the rabbit pieces to a serving platter. Garnish with lemon slices for a citrusy brightness.
5. Enjoy: Serve the Grilled Rabbit with Garlic hot, accompanied by your favorite side dishes or a simple salad. Revel in the smoky aroma and succulent flavors reminiscent of the Spanish countryside.

Nutrition Information:
(Per serving)
- Calories: 320
- Protein: 38g
- Carbohydrates: 3g
- Fat: 18g
- Saturated Fat: 4g
- Cholesterol: 120mg

- Sodium: 120mg
- Fiber: 1g
- Sugars: 0g

Note: Nutrition information is approximate and may vary based on specific ingredients and cooking methods.

53. Charcoal-Grilled Venison

Inspired by the culinary excellence of Restaurant Asador Etxebarri in Axpe, Spain, this Charcoal-Grilled Venison recipe brings the rustic charm of open-fire cooking to your kitchen. Asador Etxebarri is renowned for its commitment to using the finest quality ingredients and traditional grilling techniques, and this dish captures the essence of their artistry. The combination of premium venison and the smoky aroma of charcoal creates a symphony of flavors that will transport you to the heart of Basque country.

Serving: 4 servings
Preparation Time: 20 minutes
Ready Time: 2 hours (including marination time)

Ingredients:
- 1.5 lbs venison steaks, preferably from the loin
- 2 tablespoons olive oil
- 2 cloves garlic, minced
- 1 teaspoon smoked paprika
- 1 teaspoon ground cumin
- 1 teaspoon sea salt
- 1/2 teaspoon black pepper
- 1 tablespoon fresh rosemary, finely chopped
- 1 tablespoon fresh thyme leaves
- 1 lemon, sliced for garnish

Instructions:
1. Marination:
- In a bowl, combine olive oil, minced garlic, smoked paprika, ground cumin, sea salt, black pepper, rosemary, and thyme to create the marinade.

- Pat the venison steaks dry with a paper towel and coat them evenly with the marinade.
- Cover the bowl and let the venison marinate in the refrigerator for at least 1-2 hours, allowing the flavors to infuse.

2. Preparation:
- Remove the marinated venison from the refrigerator and let it come to room temperature for about 15 minutes.
- Preheat the charcoal grill to medium-high heat.

3. Grilling:
- Place the marinated venison steaks on the preheated grill.
- Grill for 4-5 minutes per side for medium-rare, adjusting the time based on your desired level of doneness.
- Ensure a nice sear on the outside while keeping the inside tender and juicy.
- Before removing from the grill, squeeze fresh lemon juice over the steaks for a burst of citrus flavor.

4. Resting:
- Allow the grilled venison to rest for a few minutes before slicing.
- This step ensures that the juices redistribute, resulting in a more succulent dish.

5. Serving:
- Serve the Charcoal-Grilled Venison steaks with your favorite side dishes or a simple salad.
- Garnish with additional fresh herbs and lemon slices for a vibrant presentation.

Nutrition Information:
(Per Serving)
- Calories: 300
- Protein: 36g
- Fat: 16g
- Carbohydrates: 2g
- Fiber: 1g
- Sugar: 0g
- Sodium: 600mg

Indulge in the rich, smoky flavors of Asador Etxebarri's inspiration with this Charcoal-Grilled Venison recipe, perfect for a memorable dining experience at home.

54. Wood-Grilled Wild Boar

Experience the rustic charm and bold flavors of the Basque Country with our Wood-Grilled Wild Boar recipe, inspired by the renowned menu of Asador Etxebarri in Axpe, Spain. Asador Etxebarri, nestled in the picturesque Basque hills, is celebrated for its commitment to showcasing the natural essence of premium ingredients through wood grilling. This dish captures the essence of their culinary mastery, offering a tantalizing journey into the heart of traditional Basque cuisine.

Serving: Serves 4
Preparation Time: 30 minutes
Ready Time: 2 hours (marination time included)

Ingredients:
- 2 pounds wild boar, shoulder or loin, boneless
- 1/4 cup extra-virgin olive oil
- 4 cloves garlic, minced
- 1 tablespoon fresh rosemary, finely chopped
- 1 tablespoon fresh thyme, finely chopped
- 1 teaspoon smoked paprika
- Salt and black pepper to taste
- 1 lemon, sliced (for garnish)

Instructions:
1. Begin by preparing the marinade. In a bowl, combine the olive oil, minced garlic, chopped rosemary, chopped thyme, smoked paprika, salt, and black pepper. Mix well to form a fragrant marinade.
2. Place the wild boar in a large resealable plastic bag or a shallow dish. Pour the marinade over the meat, ensuring it is evenly coated. Seal the bag or cover the dish and refrigerate for at least 1.5 to 2 hours, allowing the flavors to infuse.
3. Preheat your wood grill to medium-high heat. Remove the wild boar from the refrigerator and let it come to room temperature for about 30 minutes.
4. Remove the wild boar from the marinade, allowing any excess to drip off. Place the meat on the preheated wood grill, and cook for approximately 8-10 minutes per side, or until the internal temperature reaches 145°F (medium-rare) to 160°F (medium).

5. Allow the grilled wild boar to rest for 10 minutes before slicing. Garnish with fresh lemon slices for a burst of citrusy brightness.

Nutrition Information:
(Per serving)
- Calories: 380
- Protein: 40g
- Carbohydrates: 2g
- Fat: 23g
- Saturated Fat: 5g
- Cholesterol: 120mg
- Sodium: 350mg
- Fiber: 1g
- Sugar: 0g

Elevate your dining experience with the robust flavors of Wood-Grilled Wild Boar, a dish that pays homage to the time-honored traditions of Asador Etxebarri in the heart of the Basque Country.

55. Ember-Cooked Beef Tenderloin

Discover the rustic flavors of Asador Etxebarri in Axpe, Spain, as we bring you a tantalizing recipe inspired by their culinary prowess. The Ember-Cooked Beef Tenderloin captures the essence of open-fire cooking, a signature style of this renowned restaurant. Immerse yourself in the rich tradition of Basque cuisine and experience the smoky, charred perfection of this dish that elevates the humble beef tenderloin to new heights.

Serving: 4 servings
Preparation Time: 20 minutes
Ready Time: 1 hour

Ingredients:
- 2 lbs beef tenderloin, trimmed
- 2 tablespoons olive oil
- Salt and black pepper to taste
- 1 tablespoon smoked paprika
- 1 teaspoon garlic powder

- 1 teaspoon onion powder
- 1 teaspoon dried thyme
- 1 teaspoon cayenne pepper (adjust to taste)
- Wooden skewers, soaked in water for 30 minutes

Instructions:

1. Preheat the Ember-Cooking Setup:
- Prepare a charcoal or wood-fired grill for direct cooking with high heat. Allow the coals or wood to burn down until you have a bed of hot embers.

2. Season the Beef Tenderloin:
- Rub the beef tenderloin with olive oil, ensuring an even coating.
- In a small bowl, mix together salt, black pepper, smoked paprika, garlic powder, onion powder, dried thyme, and cayenne pepper.
- Season the beef tenderloin generously with the spice mixture, pressing the spices onto the surface.

3. Skewer and Cook:
- Thread the beef onto the soaked wooden skewers, securing it firmly.
- Place the skewers directly over the hot embers, ensuring an even cooking surface.
- Cook for about 10-15 minutes, turning occasionally, until the beef reaches your desired level of doneness.

4. Rest and Slice:
- Remove the beef skewers from the grill and let them rest for 5-10 minutes to allow the juices to redistribute.
- Slice the beef tenderloin into thick, succulent pieces.

5. Serve:
- Arrange the ember-cooked beef tenderloin slices on a serving platter.
- Drizzle with extra olive oil if desired and garnish with fresh herbs.

Nutrition Information:

Note: Nutritional values are approximate and may vary based on specific ingredients used.
- Calories: 350 per serving
- Protein: 40g
- Fat: 20g
- Carbohydrates: 2g
- Fiber: 1g
- Sugar: 0g
- Sodium: 600mg

Immerse yourself in the smoky allure of Asador Etxebarri with this Ember-Cooked Beef Tenderloin. Let the flavors transport you to the heart of Axpe, Spain, as you savor each succulent bite.

56. Grilled Iberian Pork

Elevate your culinary experience with the smoky richness of Grilled Iberian Pork, a tantalizing dish inspired by the renowned flavors of Restaurant Asador Etxebarri in Axpe, Spain. This recipe encapsulates the essence of traditional Spanish grilling techniques, showcasing the premium quality of Iberian pork. Delight your taste buds with the perfect balance of savory and smoky notes, transporting you to the rustic charm of the Basque Country.

Serving: Ideal for 4 servings.
Preparation Time: 20 minutes
Ready Time: 2 hours (including marination time)

Ingredients:
- 1.5 kg Iberian pork loin, boneless
- 4 cloves garlic, minced
- 2 tablespoons smoked paprika
- 1 tablespoon coarse sea salt
- 1 teaspoon black pepper, freshly ground
- 1/4 cup extra virgin olive oil
- 2 tablespoons fresh parsley, chopped (for garnish)

Instructions:
1. Preheat the Grill:
- Prepare a charcoal or gas grill for medium-high heat.
2. Marinate the Pork:
- In a small bowl, combine minced garlic, smoked paprika, sea salt, black pepper, and olive oil to create a flavorful marinade.
- Rub the marinade all over the Iberian pork loin, ensuring even coverage.
- Allow the pork to marinate for at least 1 hour, or preferably overnight in the refrigerator for intensified flavors.
3. Grill the Pork:

- Remove the marinated pork from the refrigerator and let it come to room temperature.
- Place the pork on the preheated grill and cook for approximately 12-15 minutes per side, or until the internal temperature reaches 145°F (63°C).
- Baste the pork with any remaining marinade during the grilling process to enhance the flavor.

4. Rest and Slice:
- Allow the grilled pork to rest for 10 minutes before slicing. This ensures the juices redistribute, resulting in a succulent and tender dish.
- Slice the grilled Iberian pork into 1/2-inch thick pieces.

5. Garnish and Serve:
- Sprinkle fresh parsley over the sliced pork for a burst of color and additional flavor.
- Serve the Grilled Iberian Pork hot, allowing your guests to savor the smoky essence and succulent taste.

Nutrition Information:
Note: Nutritional values are approximate and may vary based on specific ingredients used.
- Calories: 400 per serving
- Protein: 30g
- Fat: 28g
- Carbohydrates: 2g
- Fiber: 1g
- Sugars: 0g
- Cholesterol: 90mg
- Sodium: 800mg

Indulge in the unparalleled taste of Grilled Iberian Pork—a culinary masterpiece inspired by the rich gastronomic heritage of Asador Etxebarri, Axpe, Spain.

57. Oak-Grilled Ox Tongue

Discover the exquisite flavors of the Basque Country with this unique recipe inspired by the renowned Asador Etxebarri in Axpe, Spain. The Oak-Grilled Ox Tongue brings together tradition and innovation, showcasing the mastery of open-fire cooking that defines the culinary experience at Asador Etxebarri. Elevate your dining experience with this rich and succulent dish that pays homage to the region's culinary heritage.

Serving: 4 servings
Preparation Time: 20 minutes
Ready Time: Approximately 3 hours (including marination and grilling)

Ingredients:
- 2 ox tongues, cleaned and trimmed
- 1/4 cup olive oil
- 4 cloves garlic, minced
- 2 teaspoons smoked paprika
- 1 teaspoon black pepper, freshly ground
- 1 tablespoon sea salt
- Fresh herbs for garnish (such as parsley or thyme)

Instructions:
1. Marination: In a bowl, combine the olive oil, minced garlic, smoked paprika, black pepper, and sea salt to create a flavorful marinade.
2. Preparation of Ox Tongue: Pat the ox tongues dry with paper towels. Using a brush, generously coat each tongue with the marinade, ensuring an even distribution of flavors. Allow the tongues to marinate for at least 2 hours, or preferably overnight, in the refrigerator.
3. Grilling: Preheat your grill to medium-high heat, preferably using oak wood for an authentic flavor. Remove the ox tongues from the refrigerator and let them come to room temperature.
4. Cooking: Place the tongues on the preheated grill and cook for approximately 15-20 minutes, turning occasionally, until the tongues are charred on the outside and cooked to your desired doneness on the inside.
5. Resting: Allow the grilled ox tongues to rest for a few minutes before slicing. This helps the juices redistribute, ensuring a juicy and tender result.
6. Serving: Slice the ox tongues diagonally and arrange on a serving platter. Garnish with fresh herbs for a burst of color and additional flavor.

Nutrition Information:
(Per Serving)
- Calories: 350

- Protein: 28g
- Fat: 24g
- Carbohydrates: 2g
- Fiber: 0.5g
- Sugar: 0g
- Sodium: 980mg

Savor the smoky essence of oak-grilled ox tongue, a dish that captures the essence of Asador Etxebarri's culinary artistry. Enjoy this gastronomic journey that brings the flavors of the Basque Country to your table.

58. Ember-Roasted Sweetbreads

Elevate your culinary experience with the exquisite flavors of Ember-Roasted Sweetbreads, a dish inspired by the renowned menu of Restaurant Asador Etxebarri in Axpe, Spain. Asador Etxebarri, celebrated for its mastery of live-fire cooking, has inspired this recipe that transforms sweetbreads into a smoky and succulent delicacy. Immerse yourself in the rustic charm of Spanish cuisine as you embark on a gastronomic journey with this dish.

Serving: 4 servings
Preparation Time: 20 minutes
Ready Time: 1 hour

Ingredients:
- 1 pound sweetbreads, soaked and cleaned
- 2 tablespoons olive oil
- Salt and black pepper to taste
- 1 teaspoon smoked paprika
- 1 teaspoon garlic powder
- 1 teaspoon onion powder
- 1/2 teaspoon cayenne pepper
- Fresh parsley, chopped (for garnish)

Instructions:

1. Prepare Sweetbreads: Soak the sweetbreads in cold water for at least 2 hours, changing the water a few times. After soaking, remove any membranes or connective tissues. Pat them dry with paper towels.
2. Seasoning Mixture: In a small bowl, combine smoked paprika, garlic powder, onion powder, cayenne pepper, salt, and black pepper. Mix well to create a seasoning blend.
3. Coat Sweetbreads: Brush the sweetbreads with olive oil, ensuring they are well coated. Sprinkle the seasoning mixture evenly over the sweetbreads, covering them with a flavorful layer.
4. Preheat the Ember: Prepare a charcoal grill or an open flame. Let the embers burn down until they are glowing and covered with a thin layer of ash.
5. Ember-Roasting: Place the seasoned sweetbreads directly on the hot embers. Roast for about 5-7 minutes per side, or until they develop a beautiful golden crust.
6. Rest and Garnish: Remove the sweetbreads from the embers and let them rest for a few minutes. Sprinkle chopped fresh parsley over the top for a burst of freshness.
7. Slice and Serve: Slice the ember-roasted sweetbreads into bite-sized pieces and arrange them on a serving platter. Drizzle with any remaining olive oil and serve immediately.

Nutrition Information:
(Per Serving)
- Calories: 280
- Protein: 18g
- Fat: 20g
- Carbohydrates: 5g
- Fiber: 1g

Savor the smoky essence and rich flavors of Ember-Roasted Sweetbreads, a dish that captures the essence of Asador Etxebarri's culinary mastery.

59. Grilled Bone Marrow

Indulge in the rustic flavors of the Basque Country with this exquisite Grilled Bone Marrow recipe inspired by the culinary prowess of Asador Etxebarri in Axpe, Spain. A dish that celebrates simplicity and the natural richness of quality ingredients, this is a true delicacy for the adventurous food enthusiast. The smoky aroma and buttery texture of the grilled bone marrow will transport you to the heart of the Basque culinary experience.

Serving: 4 servings
Preparation Time: 15 minutes
Ready Time: 30 minutes

Ingredients:
- 4 large beef marrow bones, split lengthwise
- Sea salt, to taste
- Freshly ground black pepper, to taste
- 1 tablespoon olive oil
- 2 tablespoons chopped fresh parsley
- 1 tablespoon lemon zest

Instructions:
1. Preheat the Grill:
- Prepare a charcoal or gas grill for medium-high heat.
2. Clean and Season the Marrow Bones:
- Rinse the marrow bones under cold water to remove any excess blood. Pat them dry with paper towels.
- Season the bones with sea salt and freshly ground black pepper.
3. Grill the Marrow Bones:
- Brush the marrow bones with olive oil to prevent sticking.
- Place the bones on the preheated grill, cut side down. Grill for about 10-15 minutes, turning occasionally, until the marrow is heated through and the edges are crispy.
4. Garnish and Serve:
- Remove the grilled marrow bones from the grill and place them on a serving platter.
- Sprinkle with chopped fresh parsley and lemon zest for a burst of freshness.
5. Enjoy:
- Serve the Grilled Bone Marrow with crusty bread or toast points. Encourage guests to scoop out the marrow and spread it on the bread. The combination of smokiness, richness, and freshness is truly divine.

Nutrition Information:

Note: Nutrition information is approximate and may vary based on specific ingredients used.
- Calories per serving: 300
- Total Fat: 25g
- Saturated Fat: 10g
- Cholesterol: 50mg
- Sodium: 300mg
- Total Carbohydrates: 1g
- Protein: 15g

Elevate your culinary experience with this Grilled Bone Marrow, a dish that pays homage to the mastery of Asador Etxebarri's menu. Immerse yourself in the bold flavors of Spain, right in the comfort of your own kitchen.

60. Wood-Grilled Veal Chop

Embark on a culinary journey inspired by the renowned Restaurant Asador Etxebarri in Axpe, Spain, where the art of wood-grilling reaches its pinnacle. This recipe pays homage to the establishment's dedication to simple, high-quality ingredients and the primal method of wood-fired cooking. The Wood-Grilled Veal Chop captures the essence of rustic elegance, showcasing the natural flavors of premium veal elevated by the smoky embrace of the open flame.

Serving: Serves 2
Preparation Time: 20 minutes
Ready Time: 40 minutes

Ingredients:
- 2 veal chops, bone-in (approximately 1 pound each)
- 2 tablespoons olive oil
- 1 teaspoon sea salt
- 1/2 teaspoon black pepper, freshly ground
- 2 sprigs fresh rosemary
- 2 cloves garlic, minced
- Lemon wedges for serving

Instructions:

1. Preheat the Grill:
- Prepare a wood-fired grill to medium-high heat. Allow the wood to burn down until you have a bed of hot coals.

2. Season the Veal:
- Rub each veal chop with olive oil, ensuring an even coating.
- Sprinkle sea salt and freshly ground black pepper on both sides of the veal chops.

3. Infuse with Aromatics:
- Scatter minced garlic over the veal chops.
- Place a sprig of fresh rosemary on each chop, pressing it into the meat slightly to release its aroma.

4. Grill the Veal:
- Place the veal chops on the preheated grill.
- Grill for approximately 8-10 minutes per side, or until the internal temperature reaches your desired level of doneness.

5. Rest and Serve:
- Remove the veal chops from the grill and let them rest for 5 minutes.
- Serve hot, garnished with additional fresh rosemary and lemon wedges on the side.

Nutrition Information:
Note: Nutrition information is approximate and may vary based on specific ingredients used and portion sizes.
- Calories: 450 per serving
- Protein: 45g
- Fat: 28g
- Carbohydrates: 1g
- Fiber: 0g
- Sugar: 0g
- Sodium: 650mg

Elevate your dining experience with this Wood-Grilled Veal Chop, a testament to the culinary excellence inspired by the menu of Asador Etxebarri. Simple yet sophisticated, this dish captures the essence of the open flame, bringing the flavors of Axpe, Spain, to your table.

61. Ember-Cooked Lamb Kidneys

Embark on a culinary journey inspired by the rustic charm of Asador Etxebarri in Axpe, Spain. Renowned for its commitment to traditional techniques and open-fire cooking, this cookbook invites you to recreate the magic of the renowned restaurant in your own kitchen. One such tantalizing dish that captures the essence of Etxebarri is the Ember-Cooked Lamb Kidneys. Let the smoky aroma and rich flavors transport you to the heart of Basque Country as you master this delectable recipe.

Serving: 2 servings
Preparation Time: 15 minutes
Ready Time: 30 minutes

Ingredients:
- 6 lamb kidneys
- Salt, to taste
- Freshly ground black pepper, to taste
- 2 tablespoons olive oil
- 1 sprig of fresh rosemary
- 1 garlic clove, minced
- Lemon wedges, for serving

Instructions:
1. Prepare the Lamb Kidneys:
- Rinse the lamb kidneys under cold water and pat them dry with paper towels.
- Using a sharp knife, carefully remove any excess fat or membranes from the kidneys.
2. Season the Kidneys:
- Season the lamb kidneys generously with salt and freshly ground black pepper.
3. Infuse with Flavor:
- In a small bowl, mix together olive oil, minced garlic, and finely chopped rosemary.
- Brush the lamb kidneys with this flavorful mixture, ensuring they are well-coated.
4. Get the Ember Fire Ready:
- Set up a grill or barbecue with a medium-high heat. Allow the flames to subside, leaving behind glowing embers.
5. Cook over Embers:

- Place the lamb kidneys directly on the hot embers, turning occasionally. Cook for approximately 5-7 minutes or until the kidneys are cooked to your desired level of doneness.

6. Rest and Serve:
- Remove the lamb kidneys from the embers and let them rest for a few minutes.
- Slice the kidneys into bite-sized pieces and serve with lemon wedges on the side.

Nutrition Information:
- *Note: Nutritional values may vary based on the size of the lamb kidneys and specific ingredients used.*
- Calories: [Provide an estimate based on the ingredients]
- Protein: [Provide an estimate based on the ingredients]
- Fat: [Provide an estimate based on the ingredients]
- Carbohydrates: [Provide an estimate based on the ingredients]
- Fiber: [Provide an estimate based on the ingredients]

Indulge in the primal flavors of ember-cooked lamb kidneys, a dish that pays homage to the timeless culinary traditions of Asador Etxebarri. Enjoy this smoky delicacy with a glass of your favorite red wine for an authentic taste of the Basque countryside.

62. Grilled Chicken Thighs

Experience the rustic flavors of Spain with this exquisite Grilled Chicken Thighs recipe inspired by the renowned Asador Etxebarri in Axpe. Known for their dedication to high-quality, locally-sourced ingredients and traditional cooking methods, Asador Etxebarri has influenced this dish to bring a taste of authentic Spanish cuisine to your table.

Serving: 4 servings
Preparation Time: 15 minutes
Ready Time: 1 hour and 15 minutes (including marination and grilling)

Ingredients:
- 8 bone-in, skin-on chicken thighs
- 1/4 cup olive oil
- 3 cloves garlic, minced

- 1 tablespoon smoked paprika
- 1 teaspoon dried oregano
- 1 teaspoon ground cumin
- 1 teaspoon sea salt
- 1/2 teaspoon black pepper
- Juice of 1 lemon
- Fresh parsley for garnish

Instructions:
1. Marinate the Chicken:
- In a bowl, combine olive oil, minced garlic, smoked paprika, dried oregano, ground cumin, sea salt, black pepper, and lemon juice. Mix well to create the marinade.
- Place the chicken thighs in a large resealable plastic bag or shallow dish.
- Pour the marinade over the chicken, ensuring each piece is well coated.
- Seal the bag or cover the dish and refrigerate for at least 1 hour, allowing the flavors to infuse.
2. Preheat the Grill:
- Preheat your grill to medium-high heat.
3. Grill the Chicken:
- Remove the chicken from the marinade, allowing excess to drip off.
- Place the chicken thighs on the preheated grill, skin side down.
- Grill for approximately 6-8 minutes per side, or until the internal temperature reaches 165°F (74°C) and the skin is crispy.
- Adjust grilling time based on the thickness of the thighs.
4. Garnish and Serve:
- Transfer the grilled chicken thighs to a serving platter.
- Garnish with fresh parsley and additional lemon wedges if desired.

Nutrition Information:
- (Per Serving)
- Calories: 380
- Protein: 25g
- Fat: 28g
- Carbohydrates: 2g
- Fiber: 1g
- Sugar: 0g
- Cholesterol: 110mg
- Sodium: 560mg

Elevate your dinner experience with these Grilled Chicken Thighs, capturing the essence of Asador Etxebarri's culinary expertise. Enjoy the smoky aroma and robust flavors reminiscent of the Spanish countryside.

63. Fire-Grilled Turkey

Transport your taste buds to the rustic charm of Axpe, Spain, with this tantalizing recipe inspired by the culinary wonders of Restaurant Asador Etxebarri. The Fire-Grilled Turkey captures the essence of traditional Basque grilling techniques, infusing the meat with smoky flavors that pay homage to the restaurant's renowned expertise in open-flame cooking. This dish is a celebration of simplicity and authenticity, elevating the humble turkey to new heights of gastronomic delight.

Serving: 4-6 servings
Preparation Time: 15 minutes
Ready Time: Approximately 2 hours (including marination and grilling)

Ingredients:
- 1 whole turkey (about 12 pounds)
- 1/2 cup olive oil
- 4 cloves garlic, minced
- 2 tablespoons fresh rosemary, chopped
- 2 tablespoons fresh thyme, chopped
- Salt and black pepper, to taste
- 1 lemon, sliced
- 1 onion, sliced
- 4 bay leaves

Instructions:
1. Prepare the Turkey:
- Rinse the turkey thoroughly and pat it dry with paper towels.
- In a small bowl, combine olive oil, minced garlic, chopped rosemary, chopped thyme, salt, and black pepper to create the marinade.
2. Marinate the Turkey:
- Rub the turkey inside and out with the prepared marinade, ensuring it is evenly coated.

- Allow the turkey to marinate for at least 1 hour, or ideally, overnight in the refrigerator for enhanced flavor.

3. Prepare the Grill:
- Preheat your grill to medium-high heat. If using a charcoal grill, ensure the coals are hot and have a layer of ash.

4. Grilling:
- Place the marinated turkey on the grill grates, breast side up.
- Add lemon slices, onion slices, and bay leaves to the cavity of the turkey for added aroma.
- Grill the turkey, turning occasionally, until the internal temperature reaches 165°F (74°C). This should take about 1.5 to 2 hours, depending on the size of the turkey.

5. Rest and Serve:
- Once the turkey reaches the desired temperature, remove it from the grill and let it rest for 15-20 minutes before carving.
- Serve the fire-grilled turkey slices on a platter, garnished with grilled lemon and fresh herbs.

Nutrition Information:
Note: Nutritional values may vary based on the size of the turkey and specific ingredients used.
- Calories: Approximately 350 calories per serving
- Protein: 25g
- Fat: 20g
- Carbohydrates: 10g
- Fiber: 2g
- Sugars: 2g

Embrace the spirit of Asador Etxebarri in your own kitchen with this Fire-Grilled Turkey recipe, a tribute to the time-honored culinary traditions of Axpe, Spain.

64. Oak-Grilled Pheasant

Indulge in the rustic elegance of Basque cuisine with this exquisite recipe inspired by the renowned menu of Restaurant Asador Etxebarri in Axpe, Spain. Oak-Grilled Pheasant captures the essence of traditional flavors, combining the natural richness of pheasant with the smoky nuances imparted by oak grilling. Elevate your culinary skills and savor a dish that pays homage to the celebrated grilling techniques of Asador Etxebarri.

Serving: 4 servings
Preparation Time: 20 minutes
Ready Time: 1 hour and 30 minutes

Ingredients:
- 2 whole pheasants, cleaned and dressed
- 1/4 cup olive oil
- 2 teaspoons sea salt
- 1 teaspoon freshly ground black pepper
- 2 tablespoons fresh thyme leaves
- 1 lemon, sliced for garnish

Instructions:
1. Prepare the Pheasants:
- Preheat the grill to medium-high heat, using oak wood for a smoky flavor.
- Rub the pheasants with olive oil, ensuring an even coating.
- Season both inside and outside of the pheasants with sea salt, black pepper, and fresh thyme leaves.
2. Grill the Pheasants:
- Place the seasoned pheasants on the preheated grill, breast side down.
- Grill for approximately 15 minutes, or until the skin achieves a golden-brown color and grill marks.
- Carefully flip the pheasants and continue grilling for an additional 15-20 minutes or until the internal temperature reaches 165°F (74°C).
3. Rest and Serve:
- Allow the grilled pheasants to rest for 10 minutes before carving.
- Garnish with lemon slices for a burst of citrus freshness.

Nutrition Information:
- *Note: Nutrition values are approximate and may vary based on specific ingredients and cooking methods.*
- Calories per serving: 350
- Protein: 25g
- Fat: 20g
- Carbohydrates: 5g
- Fiber: 2g

- Sugar: 1g
- Sodium: 600mg

Immerse yourself in the flavors of Asador Etxebarri with this Oak-Grilled Pheasant recipe, a tribute to the culinary mastery that defines this iconic Spanish restaurant. Enjoy the smoky aromas and succulent textures that make this dish a true delight for the senses.

65. Ember-Roasted Guinea Fowl

Experience the rustic charm and exceptional flavors of Asador Etxebarri, Axpe, Spain, right in your own kitchen with this Ember-Roasted Guinea Fowl recipe. Asador Etxebarri, renowned for its mastery of open-flame cooking, has inspired this dish that celebrates the rich, smoky essence of ember-roasting. Elevate your culinary skills and transport your taste buds to the heart of Basque Country with this delectable Ember-Roasted Guinea Fowl.

Serving: Serves 4
Preparation Time: 15 minutes
Ready Time: 1 hour and 30 minutes

Ingredients:
- 2 whole guinea fowls, approximately 2.5 lbs each
- 1/4 cup olive oil
- 2 teaspoons sea salt
- 1 teaspoon freshly ground black pepper
- 1 teaspoon smoked paprika
- 1 teaspoon garlic powder
- 1 teaspoon dried thyme
- 1 teaspoon dried oregano
- 1 lemon, sliced
- Fresh herbs (rosemary, thyme) for garnish

Instructions:
1. Preheat your grill or barbecue to medium-high heat, ensuring there is a designated area for indirect cooking using embers.
2. Rinse the guinea fowls under cold water and pat them dry with paper towels. Rub the entire surface of each bird with olive oil.

3. In a small bowl, combine sea salt, black pepper, smoked paprika, garlic powder, dried thyme, and dried oregano. Mix well to create a spice rub.
4. Season the guinea fowls generously with the spice rub, ensuring an even coating on all sides.
5. Place a few lemon slices inside the cavity of each guinea fowl to infuse citrusy notes during cooking.
6. Once the grill is ready, move the guinea fowls to the indirect cooking area. Roast the birds with the grill lid closed, occasionally basting them with any accumulated juices and olive oil.
7. Cook for approximately 1 hour and 15 minutes or until the internal temperature reaches 165°F (74°C), and the skin is golden brown and crispy.
8. Remove the guinea fowls from the grill and let them rest for 10 minutes before carving.
9. Garnish with fresh herbs and serve with your favorite grilled vegetables or a side of seasoned rice.

Nutrition Information:
Note: Nutrition information is per serving.
- Calories: 450
- Protein: 35g
- Carbohydrates: 0g
- Fat: 34g
- Saturated Fat: 8g
- Cholesterol: 150mg
- Sodium: 950mg
- Fiber: 0g
- Sugar: 0g

Indulge in the smoky allure of Asador Etxebarri's cooking tradition with this Ember-Roasted Guinea Fowl, a dish that captures the essence of Spanish culinary excellence.

66. Grilled Duck Liver

Indulge your palate in the rich, smoky flavors of Grilled Duck Liver, a culinary masterpiece inspired by the renowned menu of Restaurant Asador Etxebarri in Axpe, Spain. This dish elevates the humble duck liver to new heights, perfectly capturing the essence of the restaurant's dedication to exquisite grilling techniques and premium ingredients.

Serving: 4 servings
Preparation Time: 15 minutes
Ready Time: 30 minutes

Ingredients:
- 1 lb duck liver, cleaned and trimmed
- 2 tablespoons olive oil
- 1 teaspoon sea salt
- 1/2 teaspoon black pepper, freshly ground
- 2 tablespoons balsamic reduction (optional, for drizzling)
- Fresh thyme sprigs for garnish

Instructions:
1. Preheat the Grill: Prepare a charcoal or gas grill for medium-high heat.
2. Season the Duck Liver: Pat the duck liver dry with paper towels. Drizzle olive oil over the liver and season with sea salt and freshly ground black pepper. Ensure the liver is evenly coated.
3. Grill the Duck Liver: Place the seasoned duck liver on the preheated grill. Grill for 4-5 minutes per side or until the liver reaches your desired level of doneness. The exterior should be caramelized, and the interior should be pink and tender.
4. Rest and Serve: Remove the grilled duck liver from the grill and let it rest for a few minutes. This allows the juices to redistribute and ensures a moist and flavorful result.
5. Optional Drizzle: For an extra layer of flavor, drizzle balsamic reduction over the grilled duck liver just before serving.
6. Garnish and Serve: Transfer the grilled duck liver to a serving platter, garnish with fresh thyme sprigs, and serve immediately.

Nutrition Information:
Note: Nutrition values are approximate and may vary based on specific ingredients used.
- *Calories:* 320 per serving
- *Protein:* 25g
- *Fat:* 24g
- *Carbohydrates:* 1g
- *Fiber:* 0g

- *Sugar:* 0.5g

Savor the extraordinary flavors of Grilled Duck Liver, a dish that pays homage to the culinary excellence of Asador Etxebarri. Perfect for an intimate dinner or to impress your guests with a taste of Spain's gastronomic finesse.

67. Charcoal-Grilled Poultry Hearts

Explore the rustic flavors of Spain with this tantalizing recipe inspired by the renowned menu of Asador Etxebarri in Axpe. Charcoal-Grilled Poultry Hearts bring a unique and savory twist to your dining experience, showcasing the mastery of open-fire cooking. This dish pays homage to the traditions of Spanish cuisine, highlighting the simplicity and authenticity that defines Asador Etxebarri.

Serving: 4 servings
Preparation Time: 15 minutes
Ready Time: 30 minutes

Ingredients:
- 1 pound poultry hearts, cleaned and trimmed
- 2 tablespoons olive oil
- 2 teaspoons smoked paprika
- 1 teaspoon sea salt
- 1/2 teaspoon black pepper
- 1/2 teaspoon garlic powder
- 1/4 teaspoon cayenne pepper (optional for a hint of heat)
- Fresh parsley, chopped (for garnish)

Instructions:
1. Prepare the Poultry Hearts:
- Ensure the poultry hearts are thoroughly cleaned and trimmed of excess fat. Pat them dry with a paper towel.
2. Marinate the Hearts:
- In a bowl, combine olive oil, smoked paprika, sea salt, black pepper, garlic powder, and cayenne pepper (if using). Mix well to form a uniform marinade.
3. Coat the Hearts:

- Place the poultry hearts in a shallow dish and coat them evenly with the marinade, ensuring each heart is well-covered. Allow them to marinate for at least 10 minutes to absorb the flavors.

4. Preheat the Grill:
- Prepare a charcoal grill for medium-high heat. Allow the charcoal to ash over, ensuring a consistent and stable heat source.

5. Grill the Poultry Hearts:
- Thread the marinated poultry hearts onto skewers. Place them on the preheated grill and cook for approximately 5-7 minutes per side or until the hearts are cooked through and have a beautiful char.

6. Serve Hot:
- Remove the skewers from the grill and place the Charcoal-Grilled Poultry Hearts on a serving platter. Garnish with chopped fresh parsley for a burst of color and freshness.

7. Enjoy:
- Serve hot and savor the smoky, flavorful essence of Spain's open-fire cooking.

Nutrition Information:
- *Note: Nutrition values are approximate and may vary based on specific ingredients used.*
- Calories per serving: 180
- Protein: 20g
- Fat: 10g
- Carbohydrates: 2g
- Fiber: 1g

Indulge in the rich culinary heritage of Asador Etxebarri with Charcoal-Grilled Poultry Hearts—a dish that captures the essence of traditional Spanish flavors.

68. Wood-Grilled Poultry Gizzards

Embark on a culinary journey inspired by the rustic charm of Asador Etxebarri in Axpe, Spain. One of the gems on their menu, the Wood-Grilled Poultry Gizzards, captures the essence of traditional Basque cuisine with its smoky flavors and tender texture. This recipe brings the warmth of the wood-fired grill into your kitchen, offering a delightful taste of Spain's culinary heritage.

Serving: 4 servings
Preparation Time: 15 minutes
Ready Time: 45 minutes

Ingredients:
- 1 pound poultry gizzards, cleaned
- 2 tablespoons olive oil
- 2 cloves garlic, minced
- 1 teaspoon smoked paprika
- 1 teaspoon sea salt
- 1/2 teaspoon black pepper
- 1 tablespoon fresh parsley, chopped (for garnish)
- Lemon wedges (for serving)

Instructions:
1. Prepare the Grill:
Preheat your wood-fired grill to medium-high heat, ensuring the flames have subsided, and you have a steady bed of hot coals.
2. Marinate the Gizzards:
In a bowl, combine olive oil, minced garlic, smoked paprika, sea salt, and black pepper. Add the cleaned poultry gizzards to the marinade, ensuring they are well-coated. Let them marinate for at least 10 minutes, allowing the flavors to meld.
3. Skewer the Gizzards:
Thread the marinated gizzards onto skewers, creating an even layer. This makes it easier to grill and ensures each gizzard cooks evenly.
4. Grill the Gizzards:
Place the skewers on the preheated grill. Grill the gizzards for approximately 15-20 minutes, turning occasionally, until they are cooked through and have a beautiful char on the outside.
5. Garnish and Serve:
Remove the gizzards from the grill and place them on a serving platter. Sprinkle chopped fresh parsley over the top for a burst of color and freshness. Serve the wood-grilled poultry gizzards with lemon wedges on the side.
6. Enjoy:
Delight in the smoky aroma and rich flavors of the Wood-Grilled Poultry Gizzards, savoring each bite as a tribute to the culinary heritage of Asador Etxebarri.

Nutrition Information:
Note: Nutritional values may vary based on specific ingredients and portion sizes.
- Calories per serving: ~250
- Protein: 20g
- Fat: 16g
- Carbohydrates: 5g
- Fiber: 1g
- Sodium: 600mg

Elevate your home cooking with this exquisite recipe, inspired by the renowned flavors of Asador Etxebarri. A taste of Spain awaits!

69. Ember-Cooked Escargot

Indulge your senses in the exquisite flavors of Ember-Cooked Escargot, a culinary masterpiece inspired by the renowned menu of Restaurant Asador Etxebarri in Axpe, Spain. This dish captures the essence of traditional Basque cuisine, blending the rustic charm of ember-cooking with the delicate richness of escargot. Prepare to embark on a gastronomic journey that pays homage to the time-honored techniques and flavors that define the culinary experience at Asador Etxebarri.

Serving: 4 servings
Preparation Time: 30 minutes
Ready Time: 1 hour

Ingredients:
- 24 live helix snails (escargot)
- 1 cup unsalted butter, softened
- 4 cloves garlic, minced
- 2 tablespoons fresh parsley, finely chopped
- 1 tablespoon smoked paprika
- Salt and black pepper to taste
- 1 baguette, sliced for serving

Instructions:

1. Preheat the Ember: Prepare a charcoal grill or open fire with wood embers. Allow the embers to burn down until they are covered in white ash, creating a medium-high heat.
2. Prepare Escargot: Clean the live snails thoroughly, removing any debris. Rinse them under cold water. If necessary, purge the snails by placing them in a bowl of water with a pinch of salt for 24 hours, changing the water periodically. Rinse again before use.
3. Garlic Butter Mixture: In a bowl, combine the softened butter, minced garlic, chopped parsley, smoked paprika, salt, and black pepper. Mix well to create a flavorful garlic butter.
4. Prepare Escargot Shells: Place the snails back into their shells. Fill each shell with a generous amount of the garlic butter mixture.
5. Cook Over Embers: Place the escargot-filled shells directly on the hot embers. Cook for approximately 5-7 minutes, or until the butter is melted, and the escargot are heated through.
6. Serve: Remove the escargot from the embers and arrange them on a serving platter. Serve with slices of baguette to soak up the delicious garlic butter.

Nutrition Information:
(Per Serving)
- Calories: 380
- Total Fat: 30g
- Saturated Fat: 18g
- Trans Fat: 0g
- Cholesterol: 130mg
- Sodium: 400mg
- Total Carbohydrates: 18g
- Dietary Fiber: 2g
- Sugars: 1g
- Protein: 12g

Indulge in the smoky aroma and rich flavors of Ember-Cooked Escargot, a dish that encapsulates the culinary magic of Asador Etxebarri. This recipe invites you to savor the essence of Spanish gastronomy, celebrating the art of ember-cooking and the unique delight of escargot in each mouthful.

70. Grilled Razor Shell Clams

Indulge your palate in the essence of Basque Country with this exquisite recipe inspired by the renowned Asador Etxebarri in Axpe, Spain. Grilled Razor Shell Clams offer a symphony of flavors, combining the delicate sweetness of the clams with the smoky perfection achieved through the art of grilling. Elevate your culinary experience with this dish that pays homage to the mastery of Asador Etxebarri's menu.

Serving: 4 servings
Preparation Time: 15 minutes
Ready Time: 30 minutes

Ingredients:
- 24 fresh razor shell clams, cleaned and scrubbed
- 1/4 cup extra virgin olive oil
- 2 cloves garlic, minced
- 2 tablespoons fresh parsley, finely chopped
- Zest of 1 lemon
- Salt and black pepper to taste
- Lemon wedges for garnish

Instructions:
1. Prepare the Grill:
Preheat your grill to medium-high heat. Clean and oil the grates to prevent sticking.
2. Marinate the Clams:
In a bowl, combine the olive oil, minced garlic, chopped parsley, lemon zest, salt, and black pepper. Toss the cleaned razor shell clams in this flavorful marinade, ensuring they are well coated.
3. Grill the Clams:
Place the marinated clams directly on the preheated grill grates. Grill for 2-3 minutes per side or until the shells open, and the clams are cooked through. Be cautious not to overcook, as razor shell clams can become tough if grilled for too long.
4. Serve:
Arrange the grilled razor shell clams on a serving platter. Drizzle any remaining marinade over the top. Garnish with additional chopped parsley and lemon wedges for a burst of freshness.

Nutrition Information:
Note: Nutritional values may vary based on the size and specific ingredients used.
- Calories: 150 per serving
- Protein: 12g
- Fat: 10g
- Carbohydrates: 3g
- Fiber: 1g
- Sugar: 0g
- Sodium: 350mg

Enjoy the rich flavors of the sea and the unmistakable touch of the grill with these Grilled Razor Shell Clams—an homage to the culinary excellence of Asador Etxebarri in Axpe, Spain. Perfect for a gathering of friends or a special family dinner, this dish is a testament to the beauty of simplicity in Basque cuisine.

71. Oak-Smoked Eel

Delve into the rich culinary traditions of Spain with this exquisite recipe inspired by the menu of the renowned Asador Etxebarri in Axpe. The Oak-Smoked Eel is a celebration of flavors, showcasing the mastery of wood-fired cooking techniques that define the restaurant's distinctive style. This dish promises to transport your taste buds to the heart of Basque Country, where the magic of oak smoke transforms simple ingredients into a gastronomic masterpiece.

Serving: 4 servings
Preparation Time: 30 minutes
Ready Time: 2 hours (including smoking time)

Ingredients:
- 4 fresh eels, gutted and cleaned
- 1 cup oak wood chips, soaked in water
- 1/4 cup olive oil
- 1 tablespoon sea salt
- 1 teaspoon black pepper, freshly ground
- 1 lemon, thinly sliced (for garnish)
- Fresh parsley, chopped (for garnish)

Instructions:

1. Prepare the Eels:
- Rinse the eels under cold water and pat them dry with paper towels.
- Using a sharp knife, make shallow diagonal cuts on the skin side of the eels to allow the flavors to penetrate.

2. Season the Eels:
- Drizzle the eels with olive oil, ensuring they are well-coated.
- Sprinkle sea salt and freshly ground black pepper over the eels, rubbing the seasoning into the cuts.

3. Set up the Smoker:
- Preheat your smoker to 200°F (93°C).
- Spread the soaked oak wood chips over the hot coals or smoker box.

4. Smoking the Eels:
- Place the eels directly on the grill grates, skin side down.
- Close the smoker lid and smoke the eels for 1.5 to 2 hours, or until the flesh is opaque and easily flakes with a fork.

5. Garnish and Serve:
- Transfer the smoked eels to a serving platter.
- Garnish with lemon slices and chopped fresh parsley.

Nutrition Information:
- (Per serving)
- Calories: 280
- Protein: 21g
- Carbohydrates: 0g
- Fat: 21g
- Saturated Fat: 4g
- Cholesterol: 150mg
- Sodium: 830mg
- Fiber: 0g
- Sugars: 0g

Indulge in the smoky allure of Oak-Smoked Eel—a dish that encapsulates the essence of Asador Etxebarri's culinary artistry. Perfect for those seeking an authentic taste of Basque Country, this recipe promises to elevate your dining experience with every flavorful bite.

72. Ember-Roasted Goose Liver

Indulge in the smoky sophistication of Ember-Roasted Goose Liver, a culinary masterpiece inspired by the renowned flavors of Restaurant Asador Etxebarri in Axpe, Spain. This dish captures the essence of traditional Basque country cooking with a modern twist. The rich, velvety texture of goose liver is elevated to new heights as it mingles with the subtle nuances of ember-infused aromas. Immerse yourself in the essence of rustic Spanish cuisine with every decadent bite of this extraordinary dish.

Serving: 4 servings
Preparation Time: 20 minutes
Ready Time: 1 hour 30 minutes

Ingredients:
- 500g goose liver, cleaned and deveined
- 2 tablespoons olive oil
- 1 teaspoon sea salt
- 1/2 teaspoon black pepper, freshly ground
- 1 teaspoon smoked paprika
- 1 teaspoon thyme leaves, fresh
- 1 lemon, thinly sliced
- Oak or applewood embers for roasting

Instructions:
1. Prepare the Goose Liver:
- Ensure the goose liver is cleaned and deveined, removing any membranes. Pat it dry with a paper towel.
2. Season the Liver:
- In a bowl, gently toss the goose liver with olive oil, sea salt, black pepper, smoked paprika, and fresh thyme leaves until evenly coated.
3. Infuse with Smoky Aromas:
- Preheat your grill or open flame to medium-high heat. Place the goose liver directly over the embers, allowing it to absorb the rich smokiness. Grill each side for approximately 4-5 minutes, or until the liver is beautifully seared and cooked to your desired doneness.
4. Garnish and Rest:
- Arrange the ember-roasted goose liver on a serving platter, garnish with thin slices of lemon, and let it rest for a few minutes before serving.

5. Serve:
- Present the Ember-Roasted Goose Liver with crusty bread or a side salad, allowing your guests to savor the harmonious blend of flavors and textures.

Nutrition Information (per serving):
- Calories: 350 kcal
- Protein: 25g
- Fat: 28g
- Carbohydrates: 2g
- Fiber: 1g
- Sugar: 0g
- Sodium: 650mg

Elevate your dining experience with the Ember-Roasted Goose Liver, a dish that pays homage to the culinary brilliance of Asador Etxebarri, where tradition and innovation converge in every mouthwatering bite.

73. Grilled Baby Octopus

Transport yourself to the rustic charm of Asador Etxebarri in Axpe, Spain, with this exquisite recipe for Grilled Baby Octopus. Inspired by the restaurant's commitment to showcasing the finest ingredients through traditional Basque grilling techniques, this dish captures the essence of authentic Spanish cuisine. The combination of smoky flavors and tender octopus makes it a true delight for the senses.

Serving: Ideal for sharing, this recipe serves 4.
Preparation Time: 20 minutes
Ready Time: 1 hour (including marination)

Ingredients:
- 1 pound baby octopus, cleaned
- 3 tablespoons olive oil
- 2 cloves garlic, minced
- 1 teaspoon smoked paprika
- 1 teaspoon sea salt
- 1/2 teaspoon black pepper
- 1 lemon, cut into wedges (for garnish)

- Fresh parsley, chopped (for garnish)

Instructions:
1. Begin by cleaning the baby octopus thoroughly. Rinse under cold water and pat dry with paper towels.
2. In a bowl, mix together the olive oil, minced garlic, smoked paprika, sea salt, and black pepper to create the marinade.
3. Place the cleaned baby octopus in a shallow dish and coat them evenly with the marinade. Allow the octopus to marinate for at least 30 minutes, allowing the flavors to infuse.
4. Preheat the grill to medium-high heat.
5. Thread the marinated baby octopus onto skewers, ensuring they are spread out for even grilling.
6. Grill the octopus skewers for about 2-3 minutes per side, or until they develop a beautiful char and are cooked through.
7. Once grilled, remove the skewers from the heat and place the octopus on a serving platter.
8. Garnish with fresh parsley and lemon wedges.
9. Serve hot and enjoy the smoky, savory goodness of Grilled Baby Octopus.

Nutrition Information:
(Per Serving)
- Calories: 180
- Protein: 22g
- Fat: 9g
- Carbohydrates: 3g
- Fiber: 1g
- Sugars: 0g
- Cholesterol: 100mg
- Sodium: 650mg

Note: Nutrition information is approximate and may vary based on specific ingredients used. Adjust quantities as needed for dietary preferences and restrictions.

74. Fire-Grilled Abalone

Discover the exquisite flavors of the Basque Country with this tantalizing recipe inspired by the renowned Asador Etxebarri in Axpe, Spain. Fire-Grilled Abalone showcases the restaurant's dedication to simple yet sophisticated culinary techniques, allowing the natural essence of the ingredients to shine. Immerse yourself in the smoky aromas and rich tastes of this exceptional dish that embodies the essence of Asador Etxebarri's menu.

Serving: Serves 4
Preparation Time: 30 minutes
Ready Time: 45 minutes

Ingredients:
- 4 fresh abalones, cleaned and trimmed
- 1/4 cup extra virgin olive oil
- 2 cloves garlic, minced
- 1 tablespoon fresh parsley, finely chopped
- Zest of 1 lemon
- Salt and black pepper, to taste
- Lemon wedges, for serving

Instructions:
1. Prepare the Abalones:
- Rinse the abalones under cold water to remove any debris.
- Using a sharp knife, carefully detach the abalones from their shells, keeping them intact.
- Clean the abalones thoroughly, removing any remaining bits of the digestive tract.
2. Marinate the Abalones:
- In a small bowl, combine olive oil, minced garlic, chopped parsley, lemon zest, salt, and black pepper.
- Place the cleaned abalones in a shallow dish and generously brush them with the marinade, ensuring each abalone is coated evenly.
- Allow the abalones to marinate for at least 15 minutes to absorb the flavors.
3. Fire-Grill the Abalones:
- Preheat a charcoal or wood-fired grill to high heat.
- Place the marinated abalones directly on the hot grill grates.
- Grill for 2-3 minutes on each side, or until the abalones are cooked through and have a smoky, charred exterior.

4. Serve:
- Transfer the grilled abalones to a serving platter.
- Drizzle any remaining marinade over the abalones.
- Garnish with additional fresh parsley and serve with lemon wedges on the side.

Nutrition Information:
(Per serving)
- Calories: 180
- Protein: 22g
- Fat: 9g
- Carbohydrates: 4g
- Fiber: 1g
- Sugars: 0g
- Cholesterol: 50mg
- Sodium: 350mg

Indulge in the smoky perfection of Fire-Grilled Abalone, a dish that captures the essence of Asador Etxebarri's culinary mastery. Imbued with the flavors of the Basque Country, this recipe promises a memorable dining experience that celebrates simplicity and sophistication on your plate.

75. Wood-Grilled Lobster Tail

Delve into the essence of Spain's Asador Etxebarri with this exquisite Wood-Grilled Lobster Tail recipe. The culinary prowess of this renowned restaurant lies in its mastery of fire, coaxing out unparalleled flavors from the freshest ingredients. Elevate your dining experience with this succulent lobster tail, imbued with the smoky allure of a wood-fired grill.

Serving: Serves 2
Preparation Time: 20 minutes
Ready Time: 30 minutes

Ingredients:
- 2 lobster tails, fresh and split lengthwise
- 4 tablespoons unsalted butter, melted

- 2 cloves garlic, minced
- 1 tablespoon fresh lemon juice
- Salt and freshly ground black pepper to taste
- Fresh parsley, chopped (for garnish)

Instructions:
1. Preheat the Grill: Prepare a wood-fired grill to medium-high heat, ensuring the flames have subsided, leaving hot embers.
2. Prepare the Lobster Tails: Rinse the lobster tails under cold water and pat them dry with paper towels. Use kitchen shears to split the tails lengthwise, keeping the shell intact.
3. Season and Grill: In a small bowl, mix melted butter, minced garlic, lemon juice, salt, and pepper. Brush the lobster tails generously with this mixture, ensuring they are well coated. Reserve some of the mixture for basting.
4. Grill the Lobster Tails: Place the lobster tails on the grill, flesh side down. Grill for about 5-6 minutes, basting occasionally with the reserved butter mixture. Flip the tails and continue grilling for another 4-5 minutes until the lobster meat is opaque and lightly charred.
5. Serve: Remove the lobster tails from the grill and transfer them to a serving platter. Garnish with chopped parsley for a fresh, vibrant touch.

Nutrition Information (per serving):
Note: Nutritional values may vary based on specific ingredients used and portion sizes.
- Calories: Approximately 200 kcal
- Protein: 20g
- Fat: 12g
- Carbohydrates: 1g
- Fiber: 0g

Indulge in the exquisite flavors of this wood-grilled lobster tail, a tribute to the culinary artistry of Asador Etxebarri. Enjoy the smoky essence and delicate taste of the sea in every succulent bite.

76. Ember-Grilled King Crab Legs

Ember-grilled king crab legs capture the essence of Asador Etxebarri's culinary prowess, drawing inspiration from their commitment to wood-fired perfection. This dish celebrates the rich, delicate flavors of premium king crab, enhanced by the smoky embrace of the open flame.

Serving: 2-4 servings
Preparation time: 15 minutes
Ready time: 30 minutes

Ingredients:
- 2 lbs king crab legs, thawed if frozen
- 4 tablespoons unsalted butter, melted
- 2 cloves garlic, minced
- 1 teaspoon smoked paprika
- 1 teaspoon sea salt
- 1/2 teaspoon freshly ground black pepper
- Lemon wedges, for serving
- Fresh parsley, chopped (optional, for garnish)

Instructions:
1. Prepare the Grill: Preheat a grill to medium-high heat (about 375-400°F/190-200°C). Arrange the grill for direct grilling.
2. Prepare the Crab Legs: Using kitchen shears, carefully cut along the length of each crab leg shell to expose the meat. Rinse the legs under cold water and pat dry with paper towels.
3. Make the Garlic Butter: In a small bowl, combine the melted butter, minced garlic, smoked paprika, sea salt, and black pepper. Mix thoroughly.
4. Grill the Crab Legs: Place the prepared crab legs directly on the grill grates. Brush the garlic butter mixture generously over the exposed meat of the crab legs.
5. Grill and Baste: Grill the crab legs for about 6-8 minutes, occasionally turning and basting them with the garlic butter mixture. The crab meat should be heated through and develop a slight char from the grill.
6. Serve: Remove the crab legs from the grill and transfer to a serving platter. Squeeze fresh lemon wedges over the grilled crab legs and garnish with chopped parsley if desired.

Nutrition Information (per serving, assuming 4 servings):
(Please note, nutritional values can vary based on specific ingredients and serving sizes.)
- Calories: Approximately 290 kcal

- Total Fat: 12g
- Saturated Fat: 7g
- Cholesterol: 140mg
- Sodium: 1600mg
- Total Carbohydrates: 1g
- Protein: 42g

Note: Adjust cooking time based on the thickness of the crab legs and the heat of the grill. The goal is to heat the crab meat through while infusing it with the smoky flavor from the grill. Enjoy this exquisite dish hot off the grill for an unparalleled culinary experience.

77. Grilled Squat Lobster

Indulge in the delectable flavors of the sea with this exquisite Grilled Squat Lobster recipe. Inspired by the renowned culinary craftsmanship of Restaurant Asador Etxebarri in Axpe, Spain, this dish captures the essence of simplicity and elegance, highlighting the natural sweetness of the lobster complemented by smoky, grilled perfection.

Serving: 2 servings
Preparation time: 15 minutes
Ready time: 30 minutes

Ingredients:
- 4 squat lobsters
- 2 tablespoons extra-virgin olive oil
- Sea salt to taste
- Freshly ground black pepper
- Lemon wedges for garnish

Instructions:
1. Prepare the Squat Lobsters: Preheat the grill to medium-high heat.
2. Using kitchen shears, carefully cut along the top shell of each squat lobster to expose the meat.
3. Gently brush the exposed meat of the squat lobsters with olive oil and season with sea salt and freshly ground black pepper.
4. Grill the Squat Lobsters: Place the prepared squat lobsters on the preheated grill, shell side down. Grill for about 5-6 minutes, until the

meat is opaque and lightly charred, turning halfway through the cooking time.
5. Once cooked, remove the squat lobsters from the grill and transfer them to a serving platter.
6. Serve: Garnish with lemon wedges and serve the grilled squat lobsters immediately, allowing diners to enjoy the succulent, smoky flavors.

Nutrition Information (per serving):
Please note, nutrition information may vary based on exact ingredients used and portion sizes.
- Calories: 150 kcal
- Protein: 25g
- Fat: 5g
- Carbohydrates: 1g
- Fiber: 0g
- Sugar: 0g
- Sodium: 300mg

This tantalizing dish embodies the essence of Asador Etxebarri's dedication to elevating simple ingredients through expert grilling techniques, delivering a dish that celebrates the purity of flavors from the sea.

78. Oak-Grilled Prawn Skewers

Elevate your culinary experience with the essence of Asador Etxebarri, a renowned restaurant in Axpe, Spain, celebrated for its mastery of oak-grilling techniques. Immerse yourself in the smoky flavors of the Basque Country with these Oak-Grilled Prawn Skewers. Perfectly seasoned and cooked over an open flame, these skewers capture the essence of Asador Etxebarri's culinary magic.

Serving: Makes 4 servings.
Preparation Time: 15 minutes.
Ready Time: 30 minutes.

Ingredients:
- 1 pound large prawns, peeled and deveined
- 2 tablespoons olive oil

- 2 cloves garlic, minced
- 1 teaspoon smoked paprika
- 1 teaspoon sea salt
- 1/2 teaspoon black pepper
- Wooden skewers, soaked in water for 30 minutes

Instructions:

1. Marinate the Prawns:

In a bowl, combine olive oil, minced garlic, smoked paprika, sea salt, and black pepper. Add the prawns to the marinade, ensuring they are well-coated. Allow them to marinate for at least 15 minutes to absorb the rich flavors.

2. Skewer the Prawns:

Thread the marinated prawns onto the soaked wooden skewers, ensuring an even distribution.

3. Preheat the Grill:

Prepare a grill for direct heat. If using an oak grill, you'll capture the authentic smokiness that defines Asador Etxebarri's dishes.

4. Grill the Skewers:

Place the prawn skewers on the preheated grill. Cook for 2-3 minutes per side, or until the prawns are opaque and have a slight char from the grill.

5. Serve Hot:

Remove the skewers from the grill and place them on a serving platter. Drizzle with additional olive oil if desired. Serve hot, allowing your guests to savor the smoky perfection.

Nutrition Information:

(Per serving)
- Calories: 220
- Protein: 25g
- Carbohydrates: 2g
- Fat: 13g
- Saturated Fat: 2g
- Cholesterol: 200mg
- Sodium: 650mg
- Fiber: 0g
- Sugar: 0g

Delight in the flavors of Asador Etxebarri's oak-grilled prawn skewers—a culinary journey inspired by the heart of Spanish gastronomy.

79. Ember-Roasted Sea Bass Fillet

Experience the rustic charm and exquisite flavors of Asador Etxebarri, nestled in the picturesque village of Axpe, Spain. Renowned for its mastery of live-fire cooking, this restaurant has inspired a dish that captures the essence of its culinary artistry. Presenting the Ember-Roasted Sea Bass Fillet—a symphony of smoky undertones, delicate textures, and bold Spanish flavors. Transport your taste buds to the heart of Basque country with this sensational creation.

Serving: 4 servings
Preparation Time: 15 minutes
Ready Time: 40 minutes

Ingredients:
- 4 sea bass fillets, skin-on
- 2 tablespoons olive oil
- 1 teaspoon smoked paprika
- 1 teaspoon sea salt
- 1/2 teaspoon black pepper, freshly ground
- 1 lemon, thinly sliced
- 1 tablespoon fresh parsley, chopped (for garnish)

Instructions:
1. Prepare the Ember Bed:
- If you have a charcoal grill, light the charcoal and let it burn until you have a bed of glowing embers. If using a gas grill, heat it to high and let it preheat for about 15 minutes. Alternatively, you can use a wood-fired oven or an open flame.
2. Season the Sea Bass:
- Pat the sea bass fillets dry with paper towels. Drizzle olive oil over each fillet, ensuring an even coating. Sprinkle smoked paprika, sea salt, and black pepper on both sides of the fillets, rubbing the seasonings into the flesh.
3. Ember-Roasting:
- Place the sea bass fillets directly on the hot embers or grill grates. Cook for approximately 8-10 minutes per side, or until the skin is crispy and the flesh is opaque and easily flakes with a fork. During the last few

minutes of cooking, add lemon slices to the embers to infuse a smoky citrus flavor.

4. Garnish and Serve:
- Carefully remove the ember-roasted sea bass fillets from the grill. Sprinkle freshly chopped parsley over the fillets for a burst of freshness. Arrange the ember-roasted lemon slices on top or on the side.

5. Presentation:
- Serve the Ember-Roasted Sea Bass Fillet on a warm platter, allowing the smoky aroma to tantalize your senses. Pair it with your favorite Spanish sides or a simple green salad for a complete and memorable dining experience.

Nutrition Information:
- *(Per Serving)*
- Calories: 220
- Protein: 28g
- Carbohydrates: 2g
- Fat: 11g
- Saturated Fat: 2g
- Cholesterol: 60mg
- Sodium: 550mg
- Fiber: 1g
- Sugars: 0g

Indulge in the captivating flavors of Asador Etxebarri with this Ember-Roasted Sea Bass Fillet—a dish that reflects the soul of Spanish culinary mastery.

80. Charcoal-Grilled Arctic Char

Discover the rich culinary heritage of Asador Etxebarri in Axpe, Spain, as we bring you a tantalizing recipe inspired by their menu. The Charcoal-Grilled Arctic Char captures the essence of the restaurant's commitment to quality ingredients and traditional cooking methods. This dish promises a symphony of flavors, with the smokiness of charcoal enhancing the delicate taste of Arctic Char. Immerse yourself in the Basque culinary experience with this delectable recipe.

Serving: 4 servings

Preparation Time: 15 minutes
Ready Time: 45 minutes

Ingredients:
- 4 Arctic Char fillets (6 ounces each)
- 1 tablespoon olive oil
- 1 teaspoon sea salt
- 1/2 teaspoon freshly ground black pepper
- 1 lemon, sliced for garnish
- Fresh parsley, chopped for garnish

Instructions:
1. Prepare the Charcoal Grill:
- Start a charcoal grill and let the coals burn until they are covered with white ash. Position the grill grates about 4 inches from the coals.
2. Season the Arctic Char:
- Rub the Arctic Char fillets with olive oil, ensuring they are evenly coated.
- Sprinkle sea salt and freshly ground black pepper over both sides of the fillets.
3. Grill the Arctic Char:
- Place the seasoned Arctic Char fillets on the preheated grill grates.
- Grill for approximately 4-5 minutes per side, or until the fish is cooked through and has a delicious char on the outside.
4. Garnish and Serve:
- Transfer the grilled Arctic Char fillets to a serving platter.
- Garnish with lemon slices and chopped fresh parsley for a burst of freshness.
5. Presentation:
- Serve hot and savor the smoky aroma and delicate flavors of the Charcoal-Grilled Arctic Char. Pair it with a crisp white wine to complement the dish's nuances.

Nutrition Information:
- *Note: Nutritional values are approximate and may vary based on specific ingredients used.*
- Calories: 250 per serving
- Protein: 30g
- Fat: 12g
- Carbohydrates: 2g

- Fiber: 1g

Embark on a culinary journey with this Charcoal-Grilled Arctic Char recipe, inspired by the esteemed Asador Etxebarri in Axpe, Spain. The simplicity of the preparation allows the natural flavors to shine, creating a memorable dining experience reminiscent of the Basque countryside.

81. Grilled Turbot with Green Sauce

Experience the culinary delights of Asador Etxebarri in Axpe, Spain, right in your own kitchen with this exquisite recipe for Grilled Turbot with Green Sauce. Inspired by the restaurant's dedication to using the finest ingredients and traditional grilling techniques, this dish showcases the simplicity and elegance of Basque cuisine. The delicate flavors of turbot, enhanced by the smoky notes from the grill, are perfectly complemented by the vibrant green sauce, creating a memorable dining experience reminiscent of the picturesque Basque countryside.

Serving: 4 servings
Preparation Time: 20 minutes
Ready Time: 30 minutes

Ingredients:
- 4 turbot fillets (about 6 ounces each)
- Salt and black pepper, to taste
- Olive oil, for brushing
For the Green Sauce:
- 1 cup fresh parsley, chopped
- 1/2 cup fresh cilantro, chopped
- 2 cloves garlic, minced
- 1 tablespoon capers, drained
- 1 tablespoon Dijon mustard
- 1 tablespoon red wine vinegar
- 1/2 cup extra-virgin olive oil
- Salt and black pepper, to taste

Instructions:
1. Preheat the grill to medium-high heat.

2. Season the turbot fillets with salt and black pepper. Brush each fillet lightly with olive oil.
3. Place the turbot fillets on the preheated grill and cook for 3-4 minutes per side, or until the fish is opaque and easily flakes with a fork.
4. While the turbot is grilling, prepare the green sauce. In a food processor, combine the parsley, cilantro, garlic, capers, Dijon mustard, and red wine vinegar. Pulse until the herbs are finely chopped.
5. With the food processor running, slowly drizzle in the olive oil until the sauce is well combined. Season with salt and black pepper to taste.
6. Once the turbot fillets are done, remove them from the grill and transfer to serving plates.
7. Spoon the green sauce over the grilled turbot fillets, ensuring each piece is generously coated.
8. Serve immediately, accompanied by your favorite side dishes or a simple salad.

Nutrition Information (per serving):
- Calories: 350
- Protein: 24g
- Carbohydrates: 2g
- Fat: 28g
- Saturated Fat: 4g
- Cholesterol: 60mg
- Sodium: 300mg
- Fiber: 1g
- Sugar: 0g

Indulge in the authentic flavors of Asador Etxebarri with this Grilled Turbot with Green Sauce, a dish that celebrates the essence of Basque cuisine.

82. Wood-Grilled Dover Sole

Embark on a culinary journey inspired by the rustic charm of Asador Etxebarri in Axpe, Spain. The renowned wood-fired flavors of this restaurant come to life in this exquisite recipe for Wood-Grilled Dover Sole. Delight your senses with the smoky aroma and rich taste, reminiscent of the authentic Basque Country experience. Follow these simple steps to recreate a dish that captures the essence of Asador Etxebarri in the comfort of your own kitchen.

Serving: This recipe serves 4.
Preparation Time: 15 minutes
Ready Time: 30 minutes

Ingredients:
- 4 Dover sole fillets
- 1/4 cup extra virgin olive oil
- 2 tablespoons fresh lemon juice
- 2 cloves garlic, minced
- 1 teaspoon smoked paprika
- Salt and black pepper to taste
- Wood chips (preferably oak or fruitwood), soaked in water

Instructions:
1. Preheat your wood-grill to medium-high heat. If using a charcoal grill, arrange the charcoal to one side to create a two-zone fire.
2. In a small bowl, whisk together the olive oil, lemon juice, minced garlic, smoked paprika, salt, and black pepper. This creates a flavorful marinade for the Dover sole.
3. Pat the Dover sole fillets dry with paper towels. Place them in a shallow dish and brush both sides generously with the marinade. Allow the fillets to marinate for at least 10 minutes to absorb the flavors.
4. While the fish is marinating, prepare the wood chips. If using a charcoal grill, place the soaked wood chips directly on the hot coals. If using a gas grill, place the wood chips in a smoker box or create a foil packet and place it on the grill grates.
5. Carefully place the marinated Dover sole fillets on the hot grill grates. Grill for 3-4 minutes per side, or until the fish is opaque and easily flakes with a fork. The wood smoke will impart a distinctive flavor to the fish.
6. Once grilled, transfer the Dover sole fillets to a serving platter. Drizzle with any remaining marinade and garnish with fresh herbs, if desired.
7. Serve the Wood-Grilled Dover Sole hot, accompanied by your favorite side dishes or a simple salad.

Nutrition Information:
Note: Nutritional values are approximate and may vary based on specific ingredients used.

- Calories per serving: 250
- Protein: 28g
- Fat: 14g
- Carbohydrates: 2g
- Fiber: 1g
- Sugar: 0g
- Sodium: 400mg

Indulge in the smoky perfection of Wood-Grilled Dover Sole, a culinary homage to the exceptional flavors of Asador Etxebarri. This dish invites you to savor the essence of Basque Country cuisine, bringing the warmth and authenticity of Axpe, Spain, to your own table.

83. Ember-Cooked Halibut

Experience the rustic charm and culinary excellence of Asador Etxebarri, nestled in the heart of Axpe, Spain. Renowned for its focus on live-fire cooking, this recipe draws inspiration from the restaurant's mastery of ember-cooked delights. Allow the smoky essence of the embers to elevate the delicate flavors of halibut in a dish that embodies the essence of Asador Etxebarri.

Serving: 4 servings
Preparation Time: 20 minutes
Ready Time: 45 minutes

Ingredients:
- 4 halibut fillets (6 ounces each)
- 1/4 cup extra virgin olive oil
- 1 teaspoon sea salt
- 1/2 teaspoon freshly ground black pepper
- 1 lemon, sliced for garnish
- Fresh parsley, chopped for garnish

Instructions:
1. Prepare the Ember Bed:
- If using a grill, light the charcoal and let it burn until covered with white ash.

- For an open flame, let the wood burn down until you have a bed of glowing embers.
2. Season the Halibut:
- Drizzle the halibut fillets with olive oil, ensuring they are evenly coated.
- Sprinkle sea salt and freshly ground black pepper over both sides of the fillets.
3. Place on Ember Bed:
- Carefully place the seasoned halibut fillets directly onto the bed of embers.
4. Cooking on Embers:
- Cook the halibut for approximately 4-6 minutes per side, depending on the thickness of the fillets.
- Rotate the fillets halfway through the cooking time to ensure even cooking.
- The halibut is done when it easily flakes with a fork and has a beautiful smoky char.
5. Serve:
- Gently transfer the ember-cooked halibut to a serving platter.
- Garnish with sliced lemon and chopped fresh parsley.

Nutrition Information:
- *Note: Nutritional values may vary based on specific ingredients and serving sizes.*
- Calories: XXX per serving
- Protein: XXX g
- Fat: XXX g
- Carbohydrates: XXX g
- Fiber: XXX g
- Sugar: XXX g
- Sodium: XXX mg

Enjoy the Ember-Cooked Halibut, a culinary journey inspired by the mastery of Asador Etxebarri. Let the smoky flavors transport you to the heart of Axpe, Spain, with every delightful bite.

84. Grilled Red Mullet Fillet

Inspired by the culinary excellence of Asador Etxebarri in Axpe, Spain, this Grilled Red Mullet Fillet recipe captures the essence of traditional

Basque cuisine. Known for its commitment to using the finest local ingredients, Asador Etxebarri elevates simple dishes to extraordinary heights through the art of grilling. In this recipe, the delicate flavor of red mullet fillets takes center stage, enhanced by the smoky nuances imparted by the grill. Prepare to embark on a culinary journey that celebrates simplicity, quality, and the rich gastronomic heritage of the Basque region.

Serving: Serves 4
Preparation Time: 15 minutes
Ready Time: 30 minutes

Ingredients:
- 4 red mullet fillets
- 2 tablespoons olive oil
- 1 lemon, thinly sliced
- Salt and black pepper to taste
- Fresh parsley, chopped (for garnish)

Instructions:
1. Preheat the Grill:
- Prepare a charcoal or gas grill to medium-high heat. Ensure the grates are clean and well-oiled to prevent sticking.
2. Prepare the Red Mullet Fillets:
- Pat the red mullet fillets dry with paper towels.
- Brush the fillets with olive oil, ensuring they are evenly coated.
- Season both sides with salt and black pepper.
3. Grilling:
- Place the red mullet fillets on the preheated grill, skin side down.
- Grill for approximately 4-5 minutes on each side, or until the fish is cooked through and has a lightly charred exterior.
- During the last couple of minutes of grilling, add lemon slices to the grill to lightly char and release their juices.
4. Serve:
- Transfer the grilled red mullet fillets to a serving platter.
- Arrange the charred lemon slices on top.
- Garnish with fresh chopped parsley.

Nutrition Information:

- *(Note: Nutritional values may vary based on specific ingredients and cooking methods. The following values are approximate per serving.)*
- Calories: 220
- Protein: 28g
- Fat: 11g
- Carbohydrates: 2g
- Fiber: 1g
- Sugar: 0g
- Sodium: 300mg

Note:
Asador Etxebarri's commitment to simplicity and quality shines through in this Grilled Red Mullet Fillet recipe. Enjoy the harmony of flavors and the essence of the grill, reminiscent of the exceptional dining experience at Asador Etxebarri in Axpe, Spain.

85. Fire-Grilled Swordfish

Embark on a culinary journey inspired by the renowned Restaurant Asador Etxebarri in Axpe, Spain. Immerse yourself in the smoky essence of their rustic charm with this tantalizing recipe for Fire-Grilled Swordfish. Asador Etxebarri is celebrated for its commitment to grilling over carefully selected wood, elevating the flavors of every dish. This dish captures the essence of their expertise, offering a symphony of fire-kissed aromas and exquisite taste. Prepare to elevate your dining experience with this exceptional Fire-Grilled Swordfish.

Serving: 4 servings
Preparation Time: 15 minutes
Ready Time: 30 minutes

Ingredients:
- 4 swordfish steaks (about 6 ounces each)
- 2 tablespoons olive oil
- 2 cloves garlic, minced
- 1 teaspoon smoked paprika
- 1 teaspoon sea salt
- 1/2 teaspoon black pepper
- 1 lemon, sliced (for garnish)

- Fresh parsley, chopped (for garnish)

Instructions:
1. Preheat the Grill: Prepare your grill for direct grilling over medium-high heat. If using a charcoal grill, ensure the coals are hot and covered with a thin layer of ash.
2. Marinate the Swordfish: In a small bowl, combine olive oil, minced garlic, smoked paprika, sea salt, and black pepper. Brush the swordfish steaks generously with the marinade, ensuring an even coating on both sides.
3. Grill the Swordfish: Place the marinated swordfish steaks directly on the grill grates. Grill for 4-5 minutes per side, or until the fish is opaque and easily flakes with a fork. The edges should be slightly charred, imparting a delightful smokiness.
4. Garnish and Serve: Transfer the grilled swordfish to a serving platter. Garnish with lemon slices and freshly chopped parsley for a burst of freshness. Serve immediately, allowing the flavors to shine.

Nutrition Information:
(Per Serving)
- Calories: 280 kcal
- Protein: 30g
- Fat: 16g
- Carbohydrates: 2g
- Fiber: 1g
- Sugars: 0g
- Cholesterol: 65mg
- Sodium: 650mg

Elevate your dining experience with this Fire-Grilled Swordfish recipe inspired by the culinary excellence of Restaurant Asador Etxebarri. Embrace the smoky allure of Spain's traditional grilling techniques and savor the rich flavors that define this extraordinary dish.

86. Ember-Roasted Haddock

Indulge your senses in the rustic charm of Spain with this Ember-Roasted Haddock recipe, inspired by the culinary mastery of Restaurant Asador Etxebarri in Axpe. Asador Etxebarri, renowned for its emphasis on wood-fired cooking, elevates the humble haddock to new heights by infusing it with the smoky essence of ember-roasting. Immerse yourself in the flavors of Axpe as you embark on a gastronomic journey with this delectable dish.

Serving: 4 servings
Preparation Time: 15 minutes
Ready Time: 40 minutes

Ingredients:
- 4 fresh haddock fillets
- 1/4 cup extra-virgin olive oil
- 2 cloves garlic, minced
- 1 teaspoon smoked paprika
- 1 teaspoon sea salt
- 1/2 teaspoon black pepper
- Zest of 1 lemon
- Fresh parsley, chopped (for garnish)

Instructions:
1. Prepare the Ember Bed: Start by igniting a bed of high-quality hardwood embers in your grill or fire pit. Allow the embers to burn down until they are covered in a fine white ash.
2. Marinate the Haddock: In a small bowl, combine the olive oil, minced garlic, smoked paprika, sea salt, black pepper, and lemon zest. Brush the haddock fillets generously with the marinade, ensuring they are evenly coated on both sides.
3. Ember-Roasting: Place the marinated haddock fillets directly on the hot embers, ensuring they are spaced apart. Roast for approximately 5-7 minutes per side, or until the fish flakes easily with a fork and has a beautiful golden crust.
4. Serve: Carefully remove the ember-roasted haddock from the grill, placing each fillet on a serving platter. Garnish with fresh chopped parsley for a burst of color and added freshness.
5. Enjoy: Serve the ember-roasted haddock hot, allowing the smoky aroma to entice your taste buds. Pair it with a side of grilled vegetables or a light salad to complement the dish's robust flavors.

Nutrition Information:

Note: Nutrition values are approximate and may vary based on specific ingredients used.
- Calories: 280 per serving
- Protein: 25g
- Fat: 18g
- Carbohydrates: 2g
- Fiber: 1g
- Sugar: 0g
- Sodium: 650mg

Elevate your home cooking with the essence of Asador Etxebarri, and savor the taste of Spain with this Ember-Roasted Haddock.

87. Oak-Grilled Pike Perch

Discover the essence of Basque Country cuisine with our Oak-Grilled Pike Perch recipe inspired by the renowned menu of Asador Etxebarri in Axpe, Spain. This dish captures the smoky flavors and culinary craftsmanship that make Asador Etxebarri a celebrated gastronomic destination. Oak-grilling imparts a unique, earthy aroma to the delicate pike perch, elevating it to a culinary masterpiece. Immerse yourself in the rich flavors of Spain with this exceptional dish that pays homage to the traditions of Asador Etxebarri.

Serving: 4 servings
Preparation Time: 20 minutes
Ready Time: 30 minutes

Ingredients:
- 4 pike perch fillets (about 6 ounces each)
- Salt, to taste
- Freshly ground black pepper, to taste
- Olive oil, for brushing
- Oak wood chips, soaked in water for 30 minutes

Instructions:
1. Prepare the Grill:

- Preheat your grill to medium-high heat. If using a charcoal grill, set up for indirect grilling. Add the soaked oak wood chips to the charcoal or smoker box for a smoky flavor.

2. Season the Pike Perch:
- Pat the pike perch fillets dry with paper towels. Season both sides with salt and freshly ground black pepper.

3. Brush with Olive Oil:
- Lightly brush both sides of the pike perch fillets with olive oil. This helps prevent sticking and adds a subtle richness to the fish.

4. Grill the Pike Perch:
- Place the pike perch fillets on the preheated grill over indirect heat. Close the lid and grill for about 5-7 minutes per side or until the fish is opaque and easily flakes with a fork. During the last few minutes, move the fillets to direct heat to get a slight char.

5. Serve:
- Remove the oak-grilled pike perch from the grill and let it rest for a few minutes. Serve hot, garnished with fresh herbs if desired.

Nutrition Information:
(Per Serving)
- Calories: 250
- Protein: 30g
- Fat: 12g
- Carbohydrates: 2g
- Fiber: 1g
- Sugar: 0g
- Cholesterol: 80mg
- Sodium: 350mg

Immerse yourself in the flavors of Spain with this Oak-Grilled Pike Perch recipe, a tribute to the culinary excellence of Asador Etxebarri. Enjoy the smoky goodness and delicate texture of this dish that brings the essence of Axpe to your table.

88. Grilled Zander Fillet

Embark on a culinary journey inspired by the rustic charm of Asador Etxebarri in Axpe, Spain. Renowned for its focus on simplicity and exceptional quality, this cookbook brings you a collection of 99 food ideas that pay homage to the menu of this esteemed restaurant. One such gem is the Grilled Zander Fillet, a dish that captures the essence of Asador Etxebarri's commitment to highlighting the natural flavors of the finest ingredients.

Serving: 4 servings
Preparation Time: 15 minutes
Ready Time: 30 minutes

Ingredients:
- 4 Zander fillets
- 2 tablespoons olive oil
- 1 teaspoon sea salt
- 1/2 teaspoon black pepper
- 1 lemon, sliced for garnish
- Fresh herbs (such as parsley or dill) for garnish

Instructions:
1. Preheat the Grill: Prepare your grill for medium-high heat.
2. Prepare the Zander Fillets: Pat the Zander fillets dry with paper towels. Brush both sides of each fillet with olive oil and season with sea salt and black pepper.
3. Grill the Fillets: Place the Zander fillets on the preheated grill. Grill for 4-5 minutes per side or until the fish flakes easily with a fork and has a golden brown crust.
4. Garnish and Serve: Remove the grilled Zander fillets from the grill and transfer them to a serving platter. Garnish with lemon slices and fresh herbs.
5. Serve Warm: Serve the Grilled Zander Fillet warm, allowing the natural flavors to shine through.

Nutrition Information:
Note: Nutrition values are approximate and may vary based on specific ingredients used.
- Calories: 250 per serving
- Protein: 30g
- Fat: 12g
- Carbohydrates: 2g
- Fiber: 1g
- Sugar: 0g

- Sodium: 600mg

Elevate your dining experience with this Grilled Zander Fillet, inspired by the culinary excellence of Asador Etxebarri. Simple yet sophisticated, it's a testament to the restaurant's commitment to celebrating the essence of each ingredient. Enjoy the flavors of Axpe, Spain, in the comfort of your own home.

89. Charcoal-Grilled Salmon Roe

Indulge your taste buds in the sublime flavors inspired by the renowned Restaurant Asador Etxebarri in Axpe, Spain, with our exquisite recipe for Charcoal-Grilled Salmon Roe. This dish captures the essence of the restaurant's commitment to using premium ingredients and traditional grilling techniques to create an unforgettable culinary experience. Elevate your dining moments with the smoky allure of charcoal-grilled salmon roe, a dish that pays homage to the culinary mastery of Asador Etxebarri.

Serving: Ideal for 4 servings
Preparation Time: 20 minutes
Ready Time: 30 minutes

Ingredients:
- 1/2 pound fresh salmon roe
- 1 tablespoon olive oil
- 1 teaspoon sea salt
- 1/2 teaspoon freshly ground black pepper
- Lemon wedges for garnish

Instructions:
1. Prepare the Charcoal Grill:
- Start a charcoal grill and allow the coals to ash over, providing a medium-high heat.
2. Prep the Salmon Roe:
- Rinse the fresh salmon roe under cold water and pat them dry with a paper towel.
3. Season the Roe:
- In a bowl, gently toss the salmon roe with olive oil, sea salt, and freshly ground black pepper until evenly coated.

4. Grill the Salmon Roe:
- Place a grill basket on the preheated charcoal grill.
- Carefully spread the seasoned salmon roe on the grill basket, ensuring an even layer.
- Grill the roe for about 5-7 minutes, or until they are lightly charred and have a smoky aroma. Use a spatula to gently turn them halfway through the grilling process.

5. Serve:
- Transfer the charcoal-grilled salmon roe to a serving platter.
- Garnish with lemon wedges.

6. Enjoy:
- Serve immediately, allowing your guests to savor the delicate smokiness and rich flavor of the charcoal-grilled salmon roe.

Nutrition Information:
(Per Serving)
- Calories: 150 kcal
- Protein: 10g
- Fat: 12g
- Carbohydrates: 2g
- Fiber: 0g
- Sugar: 0g
- Sodium: 600mg

Elevate your dining experience with the distinct taste of Charcoal-Grilled Salmon Roe, inspired by the culinary excellence of Asador Etxebarri. This recipe is a testament to the rich traditions and exceptional flavors that make dining at Asador Etxebarri an unparalleled gastronomic journey.

90. Wood-Grilled Sturgeon

Embark on a culinary journey inspired by the renowned Asador Etxebarri in Axpe, Spain, with this exquisite Wood-Grilled Sturgeon recipe. Asador Etxebarri, celebrated for its mastery of open-fire cooking, has inspired this dish, combining the richness of sturgeon with the smoky essence of a wood-fired grill. Elevate your dining experience with the simplicity and elegance characteristic of Basque cuisine.

Serving: 4 servings
Preparation Time: 20 minutes
Ready Time: 40 minutes

Ingredients:
- 4 sturgeon fillets (about 6 ounces each)
- 1/4 cup olive oil
- 2 teaspoons sea salt
- 1 teaspoon black pepper, freshly ground
- 1 lemon, sliced (for garnish)
- Fresh parsley, chopped (for garnish)

Instructions:
1. Prepare the Grill:
- Preheat a wood-fired grill to medium-high heat, ensuring the flames have subsided, and the coals are glowing.
2. Season the Sturgeon:
- Brush the sturgeon fillets with olive oil, ensuring they are evenly coated.
- Sprinkle sea salt and freshly ground black pepper over both sides of the fillets, gently pressing the seasoning into the fish.
3. Grill the Sturgeon:
- Place the seasoned sturgeon fillets directly on the grill grates.
- Grill for approximately 5-7 minutes per side, or until the fish is opaque and flakes easily with a fork. The wood-fired grill adds a delightful smokiness to the sturgeon.
4. Garnish and Serve:
- Transfer the grilled sturgeon to a serving platter.
- Garnish with lemon slices and freshly chopped parsley to add brightness and freshness.
5. Presentation:
- Arrange the fillets on individual plates, creating an enticing display that captures the essence of Asador Etxebarri's aesthetic.

Nutrition Information:
Note: Nutritional values are approximate and may vary based on specific ingredients used.
- Calories: 320 per serving
- Protein: 28g
- Carbohydrates: 1g
- Fat: 22g

- Fiber: 0g
- Sugar: 0g

Embrace the essence of Asador Etxebarri in your own kitchen with this Wood-Grilled Sturgeon recipe. Simple, yet sophisticated, it's a testament to the timeless flavors of Spanish cuisine. Enjoy the rich, smoky taste that embodies the spirit of open-fire cooking, reminiscent of the esteemed Axpe restaurant.

91. Ember-Cooked Cobia

Experience the rustic charm and unparalleled flavors of Asador Etxebarri, Axpe, Spain, right in your own kitchen with this Ember-Cooked Cobia recipe. Inspired by the culinary mastery of Asador Etxebarri, where the primal element of fire is harnessed to elevate ingredients to their full potential, this dish showcases the art of ember cooking. The simplicity of the technique allows the natural flavors of the Cobia fish to shine, creating a culinary experience that is both primal and sophisticated.

Serving: 4 servings
Preparation Time: 15 minutes
Ready Time: 30 minutes

Ingredients:
- 4 Cobia fillets (6-8 ounces each)
- Sea salt, to taste
- Freshly ground black pepper, to taste
- Extra-virgin olive oil, for drizzling
- Lemon wedges, for serving

Instructions:
1. Prepare the Ember Bed: If using a charcoal grill, light the charcoal and let it burn until covered with white ash. If using a wood-burning grill, let the wood burn down until you have a bed of hot embers.
2. Season the Cobia: Season the Cobia fillets generously with sea salt and freshly ground black pepper. Allow them to sit at room temperature for about 10 minutes to absorb the flavors.

3. Cooking over Embers: Place the seasoned Cobia fillets directly on the hot embers. Cook for approximately 2-3 minutes per side, depending on the thickness of the fillets. The goal is to achieve a smoky flavor and a beautiful sear on the outside while keeping the fish moist on the inside.
4. Drizzle with Olive Oil: Once the Cobia is cooked to perfection, remove it from the embers and transfer it to a serving platter. Drizzle with extra-virgin olive oil to enhance the richness of the dish.
5. Serve with Lemon Wedges: Garnish with lemon wedges and serve immediately. The smoky aroma and the delicate flavors of ember-cooked Cobia will delight your senses.

Nutrition Information:
Note: Nutritional values are approximate and may vary based on specific ingredients used.
- Calories: 250 per serving
- Protein: 30g
- Fat: 12g
- Carbohydrates: 1g
- Fiber: 0g
- Sugar: 0g

Elevate your home cooking with the primal technique of ember cooking and savor the essence of Asador Etxebarri with this Ember-Cooked Cobia dish.

92. Grilled Herring Roe

Elevate your culinary experience with this exquisite recipe inspired by the renowned Asador Etxebarri in Axpe, Spain. Grilled Herring Roe, a delicacy that embodies the essence of simplicity and sophistication, promises a burst of flavors that will transport your taste buds to the heart of Basque Country. Enjoy the rich, smoky aroma and succulent texture of this dish that pays homage to the fine art of grilling, a technique perfected by the culinary maestros at Asador Etxebarri.

Serving: 4 servings
Preparation Time: 15 minutes
Ready Time: 30 minutes

Ingredients:
- 200g herring roe
- 2 tablespoons olive oil
- 1 teaspoon sea salt
- 1/2 teaspoon freshly ground black pepper
- 1 tablespoon fresh lemon juice
- Fresh parsley, chopped (for garnish)

Instructions:
1. Preheat the Grill: Prepare a grill for medium-high heat.
2. Clean the Herring Roe: Rinse the herring roe under cold water and pat dry with paper towels.
3. Season the Roe: In a bowl, drizzle the herring roe with olive oil and gently toss to coat. Sprinkle sea salt and black pepper evenly over the roe, ensuring they are well-seasoned.
4. Grill the Herring Roe: Place the seasoned herring roe on the preheated grill grates. Grill for about 5-7 minutes, turning occasionally, until the roe is lightly charred and cooked through.
5. Finish with Lemon Juice: Just before removing from the grill, squeeze fresh lemon juice over the herring roe to enhance the flavors.
6. Garnish and Serve: Transfer the grilled herring roe to a serving platter, garnish with chopped fresh parsley, and serve immediately.

Nutrition Information:
(Per Serving)
- Calories: 180 kcal
- Protein: 20g
- Fat: 11g
- Carbohydrates: 1g
- Fiber: 0g
- Sugar: 0g
- Cholesterol: 300mg
- Sodium: 600mg

Indulge in the culinary mastery of Asador Etxebarri with this Grilled Herring Roe recipe that captures the essence of Spanish gastronomy. Each bite is a celebration of the sea, fire, and the artistry of simple yet exceptional ingredients.

93. Fire-Grilled Trout Roe

Elevate your culinary experience with the exquisite flavors of Fire-Grilled Trout Roe, inspired by the renowned menu of Asador Etxebarri in Axpe, Spain. This dish encapsulates the essence of traditional Basque Country cuisine, where the art of grilling meets the delicate richness of trout roe. Each bite is a symphony of smoky, oceanic notes that dance on your palate, paying homage to the time-honored techniques of Asador Etxebarri.

Serving: Ideal for an intimate dinner for two or as an impressive appetizer for a gathering, this dish serves 4.
Preparation Time: 20 minutes
Ready Time: 30 minutes

Ingredients:
- 200g fresh trout roe
- 1 lemon, sliced
- 2 tablespoons extra-virgin olive oil
- Sea salt, to taste
- Freshly ground black pepper, to taste
- Wood chips for grilling

Instructions:
1. Prepare the Grill:
- Soak wood chips in water for at least 30 minutes to infuse a subtle smokiness.
- Preheat your grill to medium-high heat.
2. Prep the Trout Roe:
- Gently rinse the trout roe under cold water to remove excess salt.
- Pat dry with a paper towel.
3. Grilling:
- Place the soaked wood chips on the hot coals of your grill for a smoky flavor.
- Arrange a grilling basket or use a sheet of heavy-duty aluminum foil on the grill grates.
- Carefully place the trout roe on the grilling surface, ensuring they don't fall through the grates.
- Grill for 5-7 minutes, turning occasionally, until the roe is lightly charred and infused with smoky goodness.

4. Presentation:
- Arrange the grilled trout roe on a serving platter.
- Drizzle with extra-virgin olive oil.
- Garnish with lemon slices.
- Season with sea salt and freshly ground black pepper to taste.

5. Serve:
- Serve immediately, allowing guests to indulge in the rich, smoky flavor of the fire-grilled trout roe.

Nutrition Information:
Note: Nutrition information may vary based on specific product brands and quantities used.
- Calories: 150 per serving
- Protein: 10g
- Fat: 12g
- Carbohydrates: 2g
- Fiber: 0g
- Sugars: 0g

Delight your senses with this Fire-Grilled Trout Roe recipe, a culinary masterpiece inspired by the exceptional Asador Etxebarri.

94. Ember-Roasted Tobiko

Experience the rustic charm of the renowned Asador Etxebarri in Axpe, Spain, with our Ember-Roasted Tobiko recipe. Inspired by the flavors of this esteemed restaurant, this dish combines the smoky essence of ember-roasting with the delicate burst of Tobiko, creating a culinary masterpiece that pays homage to the essence of Basque Country cuisine.

Serving: 4 servings
Preparation Time: 15 minutes
Ready Time: 25 minutes

Ingredients:
- 1 cup Tobiko (flying fish roe)
- 1 tablespoon olive oil
- 1 teaspoon smoked paprika
- 1/2 teaspoon sea salt

- 1/4 teaspoon black pepper
- 1 lemon, sliced
- Fresh parsley, chopped (for garnish)

Instructions:

1. Prepare the Tobiko:
Gently rinse the Tobiko under cold water and drain well. Pat it dry with paper towels to remove excess moisture.
2. Season the Tobiko:
In a bowl, combine the Tobiko with olive oil, smoked paprika, sea salt, and black pepper. Toss gently to coat the Tobiko evenly with the seasonings.
3. Create a Roasting Bed:
Preheat your grill or an open flame to medium-high heat. Arrange a layer of embers or hot coals on the grill grate. If you're using a home grill, you can achieve a similar effect by using wood chips or a smoking box.
4. Ember-Roasting:
Place the Tobiko in a heat-resistant pan or on a piece of aluminum foil, ensuring it's spread out evenly. Set the pan directly on the embers or hot coals. Roast the Tobiko for about 5-7 minutes, or until it develops a subtle smoky flavor and a light char.
5. Finish with Citrus:
Remove the Tobiko from the heat, squeeze fresh lemon juice over it, and give it a gentle toss. The citrusy brightness enhances the smoky notes.
6. Garnish and Serve:
Transfer the Ember-Roasted Tobiko to a serving dish, sprinkle with fresh chopped parsley, and garnish with lemon slices. Serve immediately to capture the rich, smoky essence.

Nutrition Information:

Note: Nutrition information is approximate and may vary based on specific ingredients used.
- Calories per serving: 120
- Protein: 12g
- Fat: 7g
- Carbohydrates: 2g
- Fiber: 0.5g
- Sugar: 0g
- Sodium: 380mg

Delight your guests with the distinctive flavors of Ember-Roasted Tobiko, a culinary journey inspired by the iconic Asador Etxebarri.

95. Oak-Grilled Smelt Roe

Indulge your palate in the exquisite flavors of the Basque countryside with this unique recipe inspired by the renowned Asador Etxebarri in Axpe, Spain. The Oak-Grilled Smelt Roe brings together the rustic charm of oak wood grilling and the delicate essence of smelt roe, resulting in a dish that captures the essence of the restaurant's culinary mastery. Elevate your dining experience with this simple yet sophisticated recipe that pays homage to the gastronomic treasures of the region.

Serving: Ideal for 4 servings.
Preparation Time: 15 minutes
Ready Time: 30 minutes

Ingredients:
- 1 pound fresh smelt roe
- 2 tablespoons olive oil
- Sea salt, to taste
- Freshly ground black pepper, to taste
- Lemon wedges, for garnish
- Oak wood chips for grilling

Instructions:
1. Preheat the Grill:
- Prepare your grill for direct grilling over medium-high heat, adding oak wood chips to infuse a smoky flavor into the roe.
2. Clean the Smelt Roe:
- Gently rinse the smelt roe under cold water to remove any excess salt or impurities.
3. Seasoning:
- Drizzle the smelt roe with olive oil, ensuring each piece is lightly coated.
- Season with sea salt and freshly ground black pepper to taste.
4. Grilling:

- Place the smelt roe directly on the preheated grill grates.
- Grill for 2-3 minutes per side or until the roe develops a golden-brown crust and is heated through.

5. Serve:
- Transfer the oak-grilled smelt roe to a serving platter.
- Garnish with lemon wedges for a citrusy zing.

6. Enjoy:
- Serve immediately, savoring the smoky aroma and rich flavors of the oak-grilled smelt roe.

Nutrition Information:
- *Note: Nutritional values are approximate and may vary based on specific ingredients used.*
- Calories: 150 per serving
- Protein: 12g
- Fat: 10g
- Carbohydrates: 2g
- Fiber: 0g
- Sugar: 0g

Elevate your culinary skills and embark on a journey through the tastes of Asador Etxebarri with this Oak-Grilled Smelt Roe recipe. Perfect for any occasion, this dish showcases the simplicity and sophistication that defines the restaurant's renowned menu.

96. Grilled Sea Urchin Roe

Delve into the exquisite world of Basque cuisine with this delectable recipe inspired by the renowned Restaurant Asador Etxebarri in Axpe, Spain. Grilled Sea Urchin Roe captures the essence of coastal flavors, offering a tantalizing experience for seafood enthusiasts. Elevate your culinary journey with the simplicity and sophistication characteristic of Asador Etxebarri's menu.

Serving: Ideal for 2-4 people.
Preparation Time: 15 minutes
Ready Time: 20 minutes

Ingredients:

- 8 fresh sea urchin roes
- 2 tablespoons extra virgin olive oil
- 1 clove garlic, minced
- Salt, to taste
- Freshly ground black pepper, to taste
- 1 tablespoon finely chopped fresh parsley (for garnish)
- Lemon wedges (for serving)

Instructions:
1. Prepare the Sea Urchin Roe:
- Carefully open the sea urchin shells, and gently scoop out the roe into a bowl. Discard any bits of shell.
- Rinse the sea urchin roe under cold water to remove any remaining debris.
2. Grilling:
- Preheat your grill to medium-high heat.
- In a small bowl, combine the olive oil and minced garlic. Brush the mixture over the sea urchin roe.
- Place the sea urchin roe on the grill, shell side down. Grill for about 2-3 minutes until the edges start to brown, and the roe is heated through.
3. Seasoning:
- Remove the sea urchin roe from the grill and transfer to a serving plate.
- Season with salt and freshly ground black pepper to taste.
4. Garnish:
- Sprinkle the grilled sea urchin roe with finely chopped fresh parsley.
5. Serve:
- Serve the grilled sea urchin roe immediately, accompanied by lemon wedges on the side.

Nutrition Information:
Note: Nutrition values may vary based on the size and freshness of sea urchin roe.
- Calories: Approximately 80 per serving
- Protein: 10g
- Fat: 4g
- Carbohydrates: 2g
- Fiber: 0.5g
- Sugars: 0g
- Cholesterol: 60mg
- Sodium: 350mg

Indulge in the rich flavors of the ocean with this Grilled Sea Urchin Roe recipe—a tribute to the culinary excellence of Asador Etxebarri.

97. Wood-Grilled Mullet Roe

Discover the essence of Basque culinary artistry with this exquisite recipe inspired by the renowned menu of Restaurant Asador Etxebarri in Axpe, Spain. The Wood-Grilled Mullet Roe captures the smoky flavors and delicate textures that define the restaurant's commitment to simple yet elevated dishes. Embark on a gastronomic journey as you recreate this masterpiece in your own kitchen, celebrating the rich traditions of Basque cuisine.

Serving: Serves 4
Preparation Time: 15 minutes
Ready Time: 45 minutes

Ingredients:
- 4 fresh mullet roe sacs
- 2 tablespoons extra-virgin olive oil
- Sea salt, to taste
- Freshly ground black pepper, to taste
- Lemon wedges, for serving

Instructions:
1. Prepare the Wood Grill:
- Start by preparing a wood-fired grill to medium-high heat. Allow the wood to burn down to hot embers, ensuring a steady and even heat.
2. Clean and Score the Mullet Roe:
- Gently rinse the mullet roe sacs under cold water and pat them dry with paper towels. Using a sharp knife, score the surface of each sac in a crisscross pattern. This helps the roe absorb the smoky flavors during grilling.
3. Season the Mullet Roe:
- Drizzle the mullet roe sacs with extra-virgin olive oil, ensuring they are well-coated. Season generously with sea salt and freshly ground black pepper, enhancing the natural flavors of the roe.
4. Grill the Mullet Roe:

- Place the scored mullet roe sacs directly on the hot grill grates. Grill for about 15-20 minutes, turning occasionally, until the roe is golden brown and has a smoky aroma.

5. Serve:
- Carefully remove the wood-grilled mullet roe from the grill and transfer them to a serving platter. Garnish with lemon wedges for a bright, citrusy finish.

Nutrition Information:
- *Note: Nutritional values are approximate and may vary based on specific ingredients used.*
- Calories: 180 per serving
- Protein: 15g
- Fat: 12g
- Carbohydrates: 1g
- Fiber: 0g
- Sugars: 0g

Note:
Embrace the essence of Asador Etxebarri by savoring the Wood-Grilled Mullet Roe alongside your favorite wine or as part of a tapas-style feast. This dish pays homage to the Basque culinary traditions, celebrating the simplicity and quality of fresh, local ingredients. Enjoy the smoky symphony of flavors that only wood-grilling can impart, bringing a touch of Axpe's culinary magic to your table.

98. Ember-Cooked Flying Fish Roe

Embark on a culinary journey with this exquisite dish inspired by the renowned menu of Restaurant Asador Etxebarri in Axpe, Spain. "Ember-Cooked Flying Fish Roe" captures the essence of the restaurant's commitment to using traditional methods and premium ingredients. The subtle smokiness imparted by ember cooking elevates the delicate flavor of flying fish roe, creating a symphony of taste that pays homage to the Basque culinary heritage.

Serving: Ideal for an intimate dinner for two or as an impressive appetizer for a gathering of discerning food enthusiasts.
Preparation Time: 20 minutes

Ready Time: 30 minutes

Ingredients:
- 200g flying fish roe
- Sea salt, to taste
- Freshly ground black pepper, to taste
- Extra virgin olive oil, for drizzling
- Wood or charcoal embers for cooking

Instructions:
1. Prepare the Flying Fish Roe:
- Gently rinse the flying fish roe under cold water to remove any impurities.
- Pat the roe dry with a paper towel.
2. Season the Roe:
- Sprinkle the flying fish roe with sea salt and freshly ground black pepper. Adjust the seasoning to your preference.
3. Ember Cooking:
- Preheat wood or charcoal embers until they are glowing red and covered with a layer of ash.
- Carefully place the flying fish roe on a heat-resistant surface directly above the embers.
4. Cooking Technique:
- Allow the roe to cook briefly over the embers, ensuring they are exposed to the smoky heat. The goal is to impart a subtle smokiness while maintaining the roe's delicate texture.
5. Monitor and Rotate:
- Keep a close eye on the roe, rotating them gently to ensure even cooking. The process should take approximately 5-7 minutes.
6. Drizzle with Olive Oil:
- Once the flying fish roe is cooked to perfection, remove them from the embers and place them on a serving platter.
- Drizzle with high-quality extra virgin olive oil for a luscious finish.
7. Serve:
- Serve the ember-cooked flying fish roe immediately, allowing your guests to savor the unique combination of smokiness and the natural brininess of the roe.

Nutrition Information:

Note: Nutrition information may vary based on specific ingredients and quantities used.
- Calories: 120 per serving
- Protein: 15g
- Fat: 6g
- Carbohydrates: 2g
- Fiber: 0g
- Sugar: 0g
- Sodium: 800mg

Indulge in the distinctive flavors of Asador Etxebarri with this Ember-Cooked Flying Fish Roe, a dish that seamlessly melds tradition and innovation on your plate.

99. Charcoal-Grilled Lumpfish Roe

Embark on a culinary journey inspired by the renowned Restaurant Asador Etxebarri in Axpe, Spain. Known for its commitment to wood-fired flavors and traditional Basque cuisine, this cookbook brings you a tantalizing array of dishes that capture the essence of Asador Etxebarri's menu. One such exceptional creation is the "Charcoal-Grilled Lumpfish Roe," a delicacy that elevates the unique flavors of the sea with the smoky essence of charcoal grilling.

Serving: Serves 4
Preparation Time: 15 minutes
Ready Time: 30 minutes

Ingredients:
- 200g lumpfish roe
- 1 tablespoon olive oil
- Sea salt, to taste
- Freshly ground black pepper, to taste
- Lemon wedges, for serving

Instructions:
1. Prepare the Lumpfish Roe:
Gently rinse the lumpfish roe under cold water to remove any excess salt. Pat dry with a paper towel.

2. Fire Up the Grill:
Preheat a charcoal grill to medium-high heat. The goal is to impart a smoky flavor to the lumpfish roe.

3. Grill the Lumpfish Roe:
Place the lumpfish roe on a grilling basket or a piece of aluminum foil with small perforations. Drizzle with olive oil and season with sea salt and freshly ground black pepper.

4. Charcoal Grilling:
Carefully place the roe on the preheated grill. Grill for 2-3 minutes, turning occasionally, until the roe develops a smoky flavor and a light char.

5. Serve and Enjoy:
Remove the grilled lumpfish roe from the grill and transfer it to a serving platter. Serve immediately with lemon wedges on the side.

Nutrition Information:
(Per serving)
- Calories: 120
- Protein: 18g
- Fat: 5g
- Carbohydrates: 1g
- Fiber: 0g
- Sugar: 0g
- Sodium: 600mg

Note:
Embrace the simplicity and elegance of this charcoal-grilled lumpfish roe dish, allowing the natural flavors to shine. Perfect for an appetizer or a sophisticated addition to a seafood feast, it captures the essence of Asador Etxebarri's commitment to quality and tradition.

CONCLUSION

In the fiery depths of culinary artistry, where the primal dance of smoke and flame marries with the finest ingredients, the cookbook "Embers of Etxebarri: 99 Culinary Delights Inspired by the Menu of Asador Etxebarri, Axpe, Spain" emerges as a radiant beacon of gastronomic excellence. As we traverse the pages of this culinary treasure trove, we embark on a journey that transcends the ordinary, a journey that beckons us to savor the essence of Asador Etxebarri's menu in the comfort of our own kitchens.

At the heart of this cookbook lies a celebration of the timeless traditions and contemporary ingenuity that define the culinary landscape of Axpe, Spain. The genius of Asador Etxebarri, renowned for its mastery of live-fire cooking, is distilled into 99 meticulously crafted recipes that pay homage to the restaurant's menu. Each page whispers the secrets of the wood-fired grill, the intoxicating aromas, and the symphony of flavors that have made Asador Etxebarri a pilgrimage site for food enthusiasts worldwide.

As we reach the conclusion of this culinary odyssey, it is impossible not to be captivated by the richness of experiences and the sheer diversity of dishes presented within the cookbook's pages. From the primal allure of perfectly grilled meats to the delicate dance of vegetables kissed by embers, the recipes encapsulate the spirit of Asador Etxebarri, inviting us to recreate its magic in our own kitchens. The cookbook becomes a passport to Axpe, allowing us to traverse the culinary landscape with the guidance of the chefs who have honed their craft in the hallowed halls of Asador Etxebarri.

One cannot help but appreciate the meticulous attention to detail that characterizes each recipe. The author, with an evident reverence for the ingredients and techniques employed by Asador Etxebarri, imparts not just a list of instructions but a narrative that invites us to delve into the soul of each dish. The cookbook becomes a storyteller, weaving tales of the Basque countryside, the crackling of the grill, and the joyous camaraderie that accompanies a shared meal.

Beyond the realm of recipes, "Embers of Etxebarri" serves as an educational companion, offering insights into the philosophy that underpins Asador Etxebarri's culinary approach. It encourages readers to explore the nuances of fire, to embrace simplicity, and to elevate the inherent flavors of premium ingredients. In doing so, the cookbook becomes more than a mere collection of recipes; it becomes a guide for aspiring home cooks and seasoned chefs alike, a testament to the transformative power of fire in the hands of skilled artisans.

In conclusion, "Embers of Etxebarri" is a culinary symphony that resonates with the spirit of Asador Etxebarri, inviting us to partake in the magic of live-fire cooking. It encapsulates the essence of Axpe, Spain, and the culinary legacy forged within the walls of a rustic restaurant that has become synonymous with excellence. As we bid farewell to the pages filled with gastronomic delights, we are left not only with a repertoire of exceptional recipes but with a newfound appreciation for the alchemy that occurs when fire, passion, and exceptional ingredients converge on the plate. The cookbook stands as a testament to the enduring allure of Asador Etxebarri, forever igniting the embers of inspiration in kitchens around the world.

Made in the USA
Columbia, SC
09 December 2024

48800925R00089